THE HUMAN BODY

25 FANTASTIC PROJECTS

Illuminate How the Body Works

Kathleen M. Reilly
Illustrated by Shawn Braley

Nomad Press
A division of Nomad Communications
10 9 8 7 6 5 4 3 2 1
Copyright © 2008 by Nomad Press
ISBN: 978-1-9346702-5-5

Illustrations by Shawn Braley;
page 90: Florida Center for Instructional Technology (FCIT) at University of South Florida

Questions regarding the ordering of this book should be addressed to
Independent Publishers Group
814 N. Franklin St.
Chicago, IL 60610
www.ipgbook.com

Nomad Press
2456 Christian St.
White River Junction, VT 05001

Other titles from Nomad Press

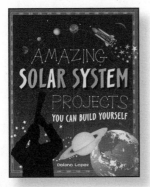

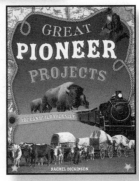

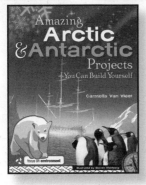

CONTENTS

INTRODUCTION

hen you look in the mirror, you see the same "you" that's always looking back. It's easy to go through your day sleeping, eating, walking, talking, doing homework—all without even thinking about it too much. But under your skin, you've got an amazing set of systems that are working together to create the life you live.

Did you know you've got a river inside of you? You do, sort of—your bloodstream. Just like a real river carries boats full of cargo up and down the waterways to their destinations, so does your blood stream, shuttling oxygen and waste products all over your body. And you've got a furnace system, too—your body can regulate its own temperature, cooling you down or warming you up so you stay the perfect temperature to keep all your systems on "go." You've also got levers (bones and joints), a highly developed computer system (your brain), and loads of chemical reactions and electrical charges. All tucked into your skin in a neat order!

EVER THINK ABOUT HOW IT ALL WORKS— AND WHAT WOULD HAPPEN IF IT DIDN'T?

Early doctors and scientists had to make some guesses about how things worked inside of us. They thought that evil spirits made you sick, while today's doctors know when you're sick, one of your body's systems is just out of whack and they can correct it. Ancient doctors meant well—they just didn't have the knowledge that modern doctors do. But they laid the groundwork for today's doctors and scientists to understand the human body.

As time passed, doctors and scientists began to realize there were things as small as germs and cells—and that our bodies were made up of billions of cells. Even today, it's amazing to think that we're walking, talking, and thinking, all because of the way trillions of cells are arranged together to create the human body. Each one of those cells is doing their job, forming your skin or creating new blood cells. Amazing!

This book will take you inside your body to get an idea about how it really works. You'll be able to create models that imitate your body's functions, and test some of those functions, too. You can take a peek inside a real heart to understand how yours is shaped and how the chambers work together to pump your blood. You can test your muscle memory and even extract DNA. When you're finished with the book, you'll probably have a completely different reaction the next time you look in the mirror. That same "you" that looked so familiar before will now look like an amazing masterpiece— a living, breathing, thinking, feeling machine that is an example of the amazing human body.

DID YOU KNOW?

Some parts of your body you can control, like your movement or your speech. But other parts function all by themselves, without you having to think about them at all, like when you're pumping blood or digesting dinner. Your body's even working when you're sleeping—your lungs keep sucking in air and releasing waste, your heart is beating, and your brain is even giving you something to dream about during the night!

CHAPTER 1
CIRCULATORY SYSTEM

Would you believe there's a river of life running through your body? **It's your blood.** Without it, your cells couldn't function at all. The path your blood takes as it moves through your body is called the circulatory system. And at the center of the circulatory system, pumping steadily, is your heart.

In cartoons, the heart is usually shaped like a box of chocolates on Valentine's Day. But it's really shaped more like a fist—and it's about the size of a fist, too. Your heart's job is to push blood through the circulatory system, transporting blood everywhere from the top of your scalp all the way down to your little pinkie toe.

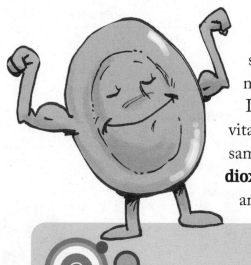

The heart is the superstar of the circulatory system, but your blood is pretty amazing too. Blood makes up about 7 percent of your body weight! It carries oxygen, sugar and other nutrients, **hormones**, vitamins, and **antibodies** to all parts of your body. At the same time, it helps get rid of waste products like **carbon dioxide**. Blood also helps regulate your body temperature and keeps your cuts from bleeding too much.

Blood travels through a maze of tubes called veins, arteries, and capillaries. They all work together so your blood can do its job—which is to keep you healthy and strong!

WORDS TO KNOW

hormones: chemicals that travel through the bloodstream to signal other cells to do their job in the body.

antibodies: proteins that help the immune system fight infections or bacteria.

carbon dioxide: the gas that's produced as a waste product by your body.

clot: the clump of blood proteins and cells that's formed over a cut to help stop the blood flow.

hemoglobin: the protein that carries oxygen in your bloodstream.

PLASMA

Just a little over half of your blood is made up of plasma. Your plasma is about 92 percent water. The rest of it is made up of proteins, dissolved salts, nutrients, and minerals. These things float around in the plasma as it transports them where they need to go. Without plasma, your blood cells wouldn't be able to move through your body.

WHAT'S IN A NAME?

Although it's easy to call the different parts of your blood by their simple names—red blood cells or platelets, for example—they also have bigger names, too:

red blood cells	erythrocytes
white blood cells	leukocytes
platelets	thrombocytes

LIFE OF A BLOOD CELL

- Blood cells are "born" in bone marrow—the stuff that's inside your bones.
- Newly made blood cells leave the marrow through blood vessels going through the bone and into the surrounding tissue.
- Blood cells spend their lives transporting oxygen and defending against intruding germs, and helping to **clot** and close wounds.
- Blood cells are short-lived—some kinds live half-a-day, others live for a few months.

RED BLOOD CELLS

Red blood cells give blood its red color. They look like flattened doughnuts (with the hole filled in). One drop of your blood contains millions of red blood cells, but they don't live very long—only about 120 days.

Red blood cells carry oxygen to other cells. First, they travel to the lungs to get oxygen. Once there, molecules inside the red blood cells called **hemoglobin** grab onto the oxygen. Then, when the red blood cells travel to a part of your body where the oxygen is low, the hemoglobin releases the oxygen for the cells to use.

DID YOU KNOW?

People make blood plasma by putting blood in a tube and spinning it around extremely fast. The force of the spinning pushes the blood cells down to the bottom of the test tube, leaving behind only the blood plasma.

WHITE BLOOD CELLS

White blood cells are bigger than red blood cells, and there are fewer of them in your blood. Even so, one drop of blood carries thousands of them.

White blood cells protect your body against foreign invaders. Whenever an infection enters your body, the white blood cells find the harmful germs and work to destroy them. Different kinds of white blood cells attack different types of infections. Some battle bacteria, others take on **parasites**, and still others spring into action in the event of an allergic reaction.

White blood cells are created in the bone marrow, just like red blood cells. They also have a short life—from half a day to a few weeks.

PLATELETS

Another element found in your blood is platelets. They are even smaller than red blood cells. Their job is to close off torn and cut blood vessels to stop the bleeding. They keep your blood where it belongs—inside of you!

Platelets help make clots and scabs. When you cut yourself, the platelets in the blood gather up around the wound. They plug the wound so it stops bleeding. After the bleeding has stopped, platelets create long threads made out of a protein called fibrin. These fibrin threads stitch together and form a mesh over your cut. This is the clot. Red and white blood cells pile up behind this mesh and, before you know it, you've got yourself a scab. The scab protects the wound until the skin completely repairs itself. But try not to pick at it!

DID YOU KNOW?

Some white blood cells are called "killer cells." Their job is to hunt down and destroy any other cells that are harming your body—like disease cells or our own infected cells.

BLOOD TYPES

Not everyone's blood is the same. Your red blood cells may carry a different protein on them than your friend's blood cells. There are four main blood types, and they're identified by the protein that rides on your blood cells. The types are A, B, AB, and O. Blood type A has A-type antigens, type B has B-type antigens, type AB has both kinds of protein, and type O has neither.

Your blood type matters if you're ever in need of a **transfusion**. If a person with type A blood receives type B blood, their body will think the B proteins are invaders and produce antibodies against it. However, a person with type AB blood can receive either A or B blood. And anyone can receive type O blood because it has neither of the offending A or B proteins. But someone with type O blood can only receive more type O blood.

DID YOU KNOW?

Platelets got their name because of the way they look—like a disc made of two little plates stuck together! When they're in action, though, they change shape and look like they have tentacles.

WHAT IS BLOOD?

You know that blood is the red stuff in your body. But there's a lot more to blood than its redness. Blood is actually made up of different parts: plasma, red blood cells, white blood cells, and platelets. Each part has its own job.

Blood cells are produced in the bone marrow, which is the soft, spongy-like substance inside bones. Inside the marrow are stem cells. These cells constantly make new blood cells to replace those that wear out. They speed up this production when necessary. For example, if the oxygen level in your body is too low, your kidneys will produce a hormone. This hormone "tells" the stem cells to start turning into red blood cells. After the stem cells turn into blood cells, they move into your bloodstream through the capillaries that run through your bones.

YOUR INNER ROADMAP: VEINS, ARTERIES, AND CAPILLARIES

Your blood moves through your body in blood vessels such as veins, arteries, and capillaries. These flexible tubes branch out like tree limbs, getting thinner as they reach the outer points of your body. Capillaries are very tiny. The capillaries in your ears, for example, are much finer than the arteries coming directly out of your heart.

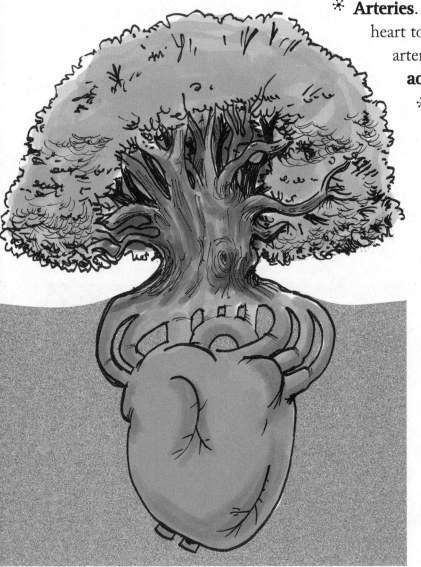

* **Arteries**. Carry blood away from the heart to the rest of the body. The main artery from the heart is called the **aorta**.

* **Veins.** Carry blood back to the heart. The main vein into the heart is called the **vena cava**.

Arteries and veins are similar in that the walls of both are made of three layers. They have a strong outer layer, then a muscle layer, and finally a sleek inner layer that allows the blood to flow easily.

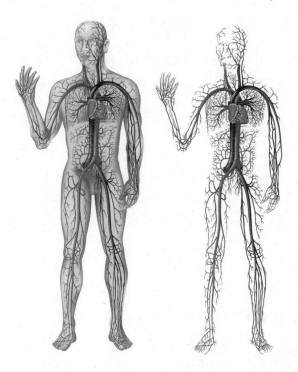

But arteries and veins are very different, too. Arteries carry blood *away* from the heart, and veins carry blood *towards* the heart. Walls of veins aren't as thick as walls of arteries, either. And there's another difference: because the heart is pushing out the blood through your arteries, the blood is flowing in one direction—away from your heart. But with your veins, the blood is on a return trip from your body, and your heart isn't pushing blood through them with the same force. So veins need valves along the way to keep the blood moving in the right direction—toward the heart. Even if you're upside down, your veins will keep moving blood toward your heart.

Capillaries are tiny with very thin walls. They're so narrow that blood cells have to line up, single-file, to travel through them. While veins and arteries transport the blood around your body, the capillaries are the tubes responsible for actually getting the oxygen and nutrients into your body tissues. That's why capillary walls are so thin—so the oxygen and nutrients can pass through them to reach your body's cells.

WORDS TO KNOW

aorta: the large artery carrying blood from the heart.

vena cava: the main vein into the heart.

AT THE HEART OF IT ALL

The heart, like your veins and arteries, has three layers in its wall, all with big names. They all have the word "cardio" in them because cardio comes from the Greek word for heart (kardia). The outer layer is called the pericardium. The next muscle layer is called the myocardium, and the smooth, inner layer is called the endocardium.

Although it is similar in shape to a fist, the heart is not just a solid block of muscle. It actually contains four hollow chambers. On the top half of your heart are the left and right **atria**. On the lower half of your heart are the left and right **ventricles**.

WORDS TO KNOW

atria: chambers of the heart that receive blood from the veins.

ventricles: chambers in the heart where blood is forced into arteries.

Here's the path the blood takes through your heart: Blood with low oxygen (de-oxygenated blood) arrives from your body into the right side of your heart through your right atrium. Then it's pumped to the lower ventricle on your right side, where it's then pumped to your lungs to pick up oxygen. At the same time, another batch of blood returning from your lungs (oxygenated blood)

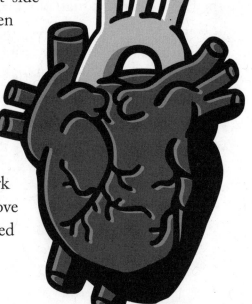

arrives in the atrium and ventricle on the left side of your heart, and the strong left ventricle then pumps it out to your body.

Between each atrium and ventricle is a valve that keeps the blood moving in the proper direction through the heart. There's also a thick layer of muscle between both sides of your heart, called the septum, which keeps the blood separated. These chambers all work with a steady rhythm, working together to move de-oxygenated blood to the lungs and oxygenated blood to the rest of the body.

BLOOD PRESSURE

Your blood is pumped through your blood vessels with a certain force from your heart. The amount of that force is called your blood pressure. Having good blood pressure is important because if it's too high (because of smoking, poor nutrition, or not exercising enough), you're making your heart work harder than is healthy for it—and you really want to keep your heart ticking for quite a long time to come!

Blood pressure is measured by figuring out how well blood squeezes through a restricting cuff (usually the blood pressure "cuff" they put around your arm to measure your blood pressure) in a certain amount of time.

Your heart beats because of an electrical impulse that causes its muscle to contract. Each heart beat has two stages. The first stage of the heartbeat is when the left and right atria contract. This moves blood into the left and right ventricles. The second part of the heartbeat is when the ventricles squeeze, pushing blood out of the heart. There's a small pause as the muscle relaxes, which allows the heart to fill up with blood again for the next heartbeat.

DID YOU KNOW?

When you were first born, your heart beat around 140 times per minute! But as an adult, it beats only half that fast!

MAKE YOUR OWN PUMPING HEART SQUIRTER

Want to see the chambers of your heart in action? With this pump system, you can see how blood flows from the atria to the ventricles, and how it's pumped under pressure out to your body. When you're ready to get it pumping, though, head outside—this project will definitely get your surroundings wet!

SUPPLIES

- scissors
- drinking straws or plastic tubing
- four small plastic drink bottles with caps
- two office binder clips
- modeling clay
- electrical tape
- water
- red and blue food coloring

1. Snip a straw into two pieces about three inches long.

2. Poke holes in the tops of all four bottle caps, and thread one piece of straw through two of the caps. Do this for both straws. Put a binder clip on each piece of straw or tubing, pinching it shut. You'll have two sets (each set will have two caps connected with one straw). Use modeling clay to plug any space around the holes in the caps where the straws went in.

3. Now you want four other straws or tubes. If you're using plastic tubing, cut two very long pieces—about ten inches long or more. If you're using straws, push one inside another until you have a very long straw. Tape them together gently. Do this twice, so you end up with two very long tubes. Be sure you don't crunch the tip of the straw too much when you push it inside the other, or else you won't have a good "blood" flow.

4. In two of the bottles, cut a hole in each of the bottoms. These will be your atria, and you're going to be pouring water in through these holes.

Atria

5. In the other two bottles, poke a hole in the top sides (near the "shoulder" of the bottles). These will be your ventricles. Thread your long straws or tubing through these side holes, pushing the straws all the way to the bottom of the bottles. Plug around the holes in the bottles where the straws enter with the modeling clay.

Ventricles

continued on next page...

MAKE YOUR OWN PUMPING HEART SQUIRTER continued

6. Screw all four caps on the bottles. Be sure your atria are at the top (upside down). Tape both the atria together with electrical tape, and tape both of the ventricles together. The tubes from the ventricles will rise up past the atria, so you may want to gently tape them against the atria so they're not flopping around.

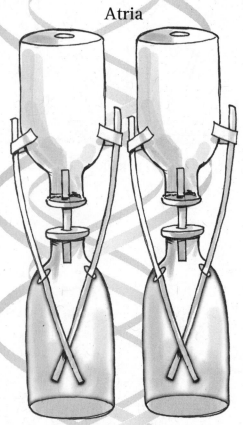

Atria

Ventricles

7. Dye one batch of water red (for oxygenated blood), and pour it into one top bottle (atrium). Dye another batch of water blue (for deoxygenated blood), and pour it into the second atrium bottle. The binder clips will keep most of the water from moving on to the ventricle bottles—just like the valves in your heart keep the blood from moving on to the next chamber.

8. When you're ready (and outside!), release the water by removing the binder clips. The water will flow into the ventricles. Then, close the valves by replacing the binder clips.

9. For the second part of the heartbeat, squeeze the bottom bottles. The "blood" will shoot out of your straws or tubing through pressure!

MAKE YOUR OWN FAKE BLOOD

If you're ever in need of some fake blood for a science experiment or crazy costume, skip the ketchup. Real blood is darker and thicker than ketchup. Instead, try this recipe for artificial, but real-looking, blood.

SUPPLIES

- 5 tablespoons cornstarch
- $1/3$ cup warm water
- $2/3$ cup corn syrup
- red food coloring
- 1 tablespoon cocoa powder
- green food coloring

1. Mix the cornstarch with the water. Stir in the corn syrup.

2. Add the food coloring slowly so you can get the color you want. For darker, more realistic blood, add the cocoa powder. Experiment with adding a little green coloring to get just the right tint.

MAKE YOUR OWN DISSECTION LAB

A lamb's heart is about the same size and shape as your heart. Ask the person at the meat counter to save you one that has much of the veins and connective tissue still attached.

Note: Adult supervision is suggested.

SUPPLIES

- disposable gloves
- baking dish or tray
- lamb heart
- sharp knife (longer ones work better) or scissors
- disinfectant

1. Put on the gloves. Using the baking dish or tray as a work surface, examine the heart before cutting into it. You may be able to see the big veins and arteries entering and exiting the heart. Take a look at how tough the heart muscle really is.

2. You may be able to identify the aorta and **pulmonary artery**, so position the heart so those are at the top.

3. Carefully cut the heart in half, top to bottom, to see the inside. Try to cut slowly, so you can get the best result. You should be able to see the atriums on the top and the ventricles on the bottom. You should also be able to see the thick septum, or dividing wall, between the left and right halves of the heart.

4. See if you can identify the valves between the chambers. Also try to see, from the inside, where the aorta and pulmonary artery leave the chambers.

5. When you're finished examining the heart, throw away the gloves and disinfect all your work surfaces.

WORDS TO KNOW

pulmonary artery: an artery that carries poorly oxygenated blood from the right ventricle of the heart to the lungs.

CHAPTER 2
RESPIRATORY SYSTEM

Every day, you breathe in and out without even thinking about it— even when you're sleeping. That's because your respiratory system is doing its job. It brings air into your lungs so your cells can get the oxygen they need. Your lungs aren't the only things working in the respiratory system, though. Your nose, **trachea**— or windpipe—and bronchial tubes all pitch in, too.

LUNGS

Along with the heart, the lungs are the big organs in our chest. The job of the lungs is to breathe in oxygen and breathe out carbon dioxide. Unlike your heart, your lungs aren't made of muscle. They consist of stretchy, spongy tissue that expands and contracts as you inhale and exhale. Your left lung shares space with your heart and is made up of two "lobes," or sections. Your right lung is divided into three lobes. Each of the lobes works the same as the others. And although your lungs are squishy and could be easily damaged, the bony cage of your ribs protects them from any harm (it protects your heart, too).

When you breathe in, you're pulling air into your body—but it's not just a straight shot to your lungs from your nose or mouth. Inside your lungs it's very moist. Bacteria and viruses love it there, and could easily create an infection in your lungs. That's why it's important for the outside air (which may be carrying unwanted guests) to pass through a series of defenses before it reaches your lungs. The air passes through a series of filtering pathways before it reaches its final destination.

DID YOU NOSE?

Some scientists estimate that when you sneeze, the air blows out of your nose at around 100 miles per hour!

NOSE

The first place air enters your body is through your nose. Of course, your nose is for smelling, but it's also an important part of your respiratory system. Your nose helps warm the air that you're breathing to help bring it to body temperature. Your nose is also lined with little hairs and sheets of sticky mucus. These things catch tiny particles of dust and bacteria and prevent them from traveling to your lungs.

If you've ever had a tickle in your nose and sneezed, it's probably because your nose was just doing its job and getting rid of unwanted intruders.

Even though you can breathe through your mouth, it's better to breathe through your nose. The mouth doesn't filter out particles in the air.

TRACHEA

You may be surprised to know that your nose is not just the nose on your face, but it also includes a big nose cavity that lies above the roof of your mouth and goes all the way back to the top of your throat. From the nose and throat, the air you've breathed in travels through your voicebox and then into your trachea, or windpipe. Your trachea contains mucus and tiny "hairs" called **cilia** that help capture any particles that made it past your nose. Small rings of **cartilage** keep your trachea open at all times. If you gently push on the front of your lower neck you can feel the stiff rings. If any little particles get caught in your trachea, you automatically cough to get rid of them.

BRONCHIAL TUBES

Your trachea branches into two tunnels, called bronchial tubes. These go into your lungs and divide into smaller and smaller branches called bronchioles. Eventually the bronchioles get so small that they're just tiny sacs of air.

DIAPHRAGM

Your lungs aren't muscles, so they can't move themselves. When you breathe in and out, your chest rises and falls. But this isn't because your lungs are sucking in air on their own. That job belongs to two parts of your body that work together.

trachea: your windpipe, the tube through which air enters your lungs.

esophagus: the long tube connecting your mouth to your stomach.

cilia: tiny "hairs" that line your trachea.

cartilage: stiff, flexible tissue that mostly converts to bone in adults.

carbon monoxide: a colorless, odorless, very toxic gas that is in cigarette smoke.

These are the muscles of your chest wall and a dome of thin muscle at the bottom of your chest called the diaphragm.

When you take a breath, both the chest muscles between your ribs and your diaphragm contract. Lay your hands on your chest, take a deep breath, and feel your rib cage expand. This expansion of the chest cavity makes the air from outside of your body rush in and inflate your lungs. When you exhale, those same muscles relax, pushing the air back outside of your body.

Your breathing is controlled by a part of your brain called the medulla. When you're running low on oxygen—or if your body suddenly needs more, like when you're exercising—your medulla will increase the speed and depth of your breathing. Now your body's cells will get the oxygen they need.

ALVEOLI

The sacs of air in the lung are called alveoli. This is where the transfer of gases takes place in your lungs. When de-oxygenated blood arrives in your heart, it's pumped through the pulmonary artery to each of your lungs. There, it dumps off the waste product, carbon dioxide, into your lung alveoli and you breathe it out. When you breathe in, the oxygen in the air hitches a ride with the hemoglobin in the red blood cells. Then, that newly oxygenated blood heads back to the heart.

HICCUP!

Everyone's had hiccups at one time or another (and somehow it always seems to happen when you're supposed to be quiet!). When you hiccup, your diaphragm spasms on its own. You can't control it. According to scientists, there are many different reasons you hiccup— laughing too hard, eating spicy foods, or eating too quickly, for example.

BREATHING OUT

You breathe in oxygen, but you breathe out carbon dioxide. Just as blood comes to pick up oxygen in the lungs, it also drops off the waste created by cells there. So even though the air coming out of your nose feels the same as the air coming in, it's really quite different.

WHEN THE BREATHING GETS TOUGH...

If all goes well, you'll probably breathe about 600 million times during your life. But sometimes people have problems with their respiratory system. Some of the problems come about because of lifestyle choices. Other problems occur because of something in the environment.

One lifestyle choice that leads to problems is smoking. As you saw, your body has defenses against intruders, like the cilia and mucus lining your nose and trachea. But there are some things that can overpower those defenses, like cigarette smoke.

When people smoke, they're breathing in **carbon monoxide** and other dangerous chemicals. Cigarette smoke damages the cilia so they're not as effective against other intruders. Also, smoke carries a brown, sticky substance called tar, which can get stuck in the lungs and cause cancer. Because carbon monoxide gets picked up by the red blood cells, these cells can't hold as much oxygen and the heart has to pump harder to supply more oxygen.

An example of something in the environment that causes problems with your respiratory system is the common cold virus. You catch this from viruses left behind by other people, or even when they sneeze or cough on you! You're probably familiar with the symptoms of a cold: sneezing, coughing, stuffy or runny nose, and sore throat. One of the best defenses against catching a cold is to wash your hands often! This gets rid of the germs.

Allergic reactions can also bother your respiratory system. Allergies are usually due to something that's floating in the air, like animal dander (dry skin and hair that falls off animals), dust mites, or pollen. If you look at pollen under a microscope, you can see why it might be irritating to people's airways—it looks like a sharp, bristly beach ball! When people are bothered by irritants like this, their bodies often react with a sneezing fit or a runny nose.

ASTHMA

A more serious reaction to airborne irritants is asthma. When people with asthma breathe in irritating things, a chemical process happens in their bodies that causes their breathing passages get narrow and fill with mucus. This makes it very hard to breathe. People with asthma can inhale medication that works to open the airways back up so they can breathe easier.

MAKE YOUR OWN MODEL LUNG

You've learned that lungs aren't muscles that move themselves. Instead, they depend on air pressure in your chest cavity and movement from your diaphragm and chest muscles to inflate and deflate. Here's how you can see this in action.

1. Cut the bottom from the bottle. Put the small balloon on the end of the straw, and secure it with a rubber band. This is going to act as one of your lungs.

2. Poke a hole in the cap, and push the straw through it up through the open bottom of the bottle. Use the modeling clay around the top to seal where the straw comes out the cap on top.

3. Cut the neck off the larger balloon, then stretch it over the bottom opening of the bottle. Secure it in place with a rubber band. This balloon will work as your diaphragm.

4. Look at the small balloon (the "lung"). It's hanging, empty, like your lungs before you breathe in. Then, gently pinch the diaphragm balloon to get a good grip, and pull down slowly. The lung balloon fills with air. When you release the diaphragm balloon, the lung deflates.

SUPPLIES

- scissors
- two-liter plastic bottle, with cap on
- straw
- one small balloon (like a water balloon)
- rubber bands
- modeling clay
- one large balloon (like a party balloon)

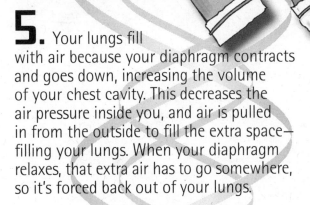

5. Your lungs fill with air because your diaphragm contracts and goes down, increasing the volume of your chest cavity. This decreases the air pressure inside you, and air is pulled in from the outside to fill the extra space—filling your lungs. When your diaphragm relaxes, that extra air has to go somewhere, so it's forced back out of your lungs.

MAKE YOUR OWN MAGIC AIR BALL

Test your lung power and see how long you can keep the ball hovering over the end of the pipe.

SUPPLIES

- bendable drinking straw
- scissors
- pipe cleaner or thin wire
- tape
- 1-inch foam ball or ping-pong ball

1. On the end of the straw nearest its bendable elbow, cut four small, evenly-spaced slits (about ½ inch long) from the tip to make four tabs. Bend the tabs back at a right angle to the straw.

2. Bend the end of the straw up at its elbow.

3. Bend one end of the pipe cleaner or thin wire, into a halo shape. About two inches down the pipe cleaner, tape the length of the pipe cleaner to the upturned straw. Try to position the halo about an inch above the hole in the straw. You can cut any excess wire off the other end.

4. Place the ball on top of the halo, then blow gently. See how much lung power you have to use to lift the ball. Then try blowing so the ball hovers over the halo. See if you can get it to come back down in its resting spot.

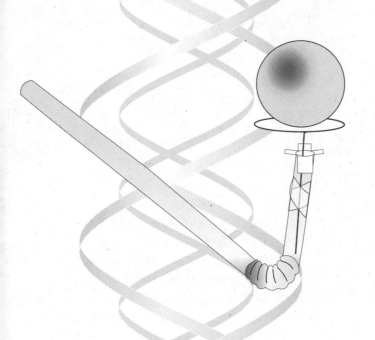

CHAPTER 3
DIGESTIVE SYSTEM

Ever wonder why that apple you ate for lunch is better for your body than the slice of chocolate cake you had for dessert? Or how your body processes any food at all? It's all thanks to your digestive system.

When you eat food, your body doesn't judge if it's "good" food or "bad" food. It just starts breaking the food down and figuring out how to get energy from it. This process of transforming the food into energy is called digesting.

WORDS TO KNOW

peristalsis: the squeezing process of moving food through your esophagus, stomach, and intestines.

pharynx: the first part of your throat, right after your mouth.

bolus: the soft blob of chewed food that you swallow.

Everything you put into your body gets processed one way or another. Your digestive tube not only breaks down food into its simplest nutrients, but it also absorbs these nutrients into your bloodstream. It leaves the undigestable parts alone, to pass as feces (when you go to the bathroom). But if you eat a lot and absorb more nutrients than you can use the body turns them into something else—fat.

LET'S GET THE PARTY STARTED

Your digestive system isn't all guts and innards. In fact, you can easily see one very important part of your digestive system—your teeth! When you bite, rip, and chew your food, you're starting the digestive process. With help from your tongue and saliva (spit), all that chomping is breaking your food down into smaller pieces. Smaller pieces make it easier for the rest of your system to extract the nutrients it needs from the food so eat slowly, take small bites, and chew your food well!

Your teeth are designed to help you tackle all kinds of food. Your incisors are the teeth in the very front of your mouth. They're for shearing off pieces of food. Your canines are next—they're the pointy ones in the front of your mouth. You use your canines for tearing food. The flat teeth toward the rear of your mouth are your molars, and you use them for grinding and chewing into smaller

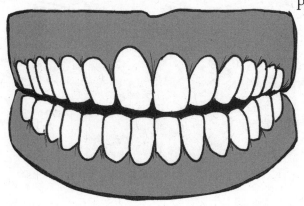

pieces. Ever swallow something that was too big, and you felt that lump in your throat? Your teeth are the first step in digestion, and your body would thank you not to forget that!

Your tongue plays an important role in the digestive process, too. Although it looks like one flap of tissue, it's actually a group of muscles banded together.

FROM TABLE TO TOILET: HOW LONG DOES IT TAKE?

After you swallow your food, how long does it take to go through the digestion process? Here's a summary:

* In about half an hour, the stomach acids begin to break down the food. The food then begins to pass to your small intestine. After about six hours, your stomach is empty again.

* Two hours after you ate, the food starts traveling down the long small intestine where most food breakdown happens and most nutrients are absorbed.

* After about 18 hours, wastes are starting to form in your large intestine. The water is absorbed by your body and any solid waste begins moving toward your rectum.

* After about 24 hours, the wastes are ready to leave your body.

DID YOU KNOW?

Even if you were upside down, your food would still move in the right direction down your esophagus toward your stomach. This is because of **peristalsis**.

These muscles place the food between the chewing teeth and then guide it to the back of your mouth to swallow.

You've also got salivary glands in your mouth that produce saliva. Saliva lubricates the food in your mouth so it's easier to chew. It also has chemicals in it that help start breaking down the food. There are three main salivary glands. There's a large one in the back of your mouth, and two smaller ones under your tongue.

After your teeth, tongue, and saliva break down your food, it passes through your **pharynx**, or throat, and begins to enter the esophagus. The esophagus is the muscular tube leading to your stomach. At this point, the blob of food is called a **bolus**, a roundish mass of food shaped from your chewing and stuck together by your saliva. Its round shape is perfect to move it easily through your digestive system—that's part of the reason it's important to chew your food well!

LET'S BREAK IT DOWN SOME MORE

Other parts of your body that play a role in the digestive system, even if food doesn't pass directly through them.

* **Liver.** Your liver—the largest gland in your body—provides your digestive system with bile, a yellow/green substance that helps break down fats. Your liver is in the upper right portion of your abdominal cavity.

* **Pancreas.** The pancreas is just behind your stomach and secretes enzymes that help digestive juices break down protein and carbohydrates.

WORDS TO KNOW

sphincter: a round muscle that opens and closes to let something pass through.

As you swallow, the muscles of the pharynx act like a clenching hand to squeeze the bolus downward. Meanwhile, the epiglottis is folding over your voicebox, preventing any food from going the wrong way, into your trachea.

Once the bolus is in the esophagus, the muscular wall of this tube moves it to your stomach by a series of rhythmic contractions. This process is called peristalsis.

The next stop is your stomach. This is a bean-shaped, hollow organ that's at the end of your esophagus. Although you may think your "belly" is your stomach, it reaches a little higher up than you probably think, and it's positioned on the upper left side of your abdominal cavity.

On top of the stomach is a ring of smooth muscle called a **sphincter**. This prevents the acidic stomach contents from squeezing up to burn your esophagus and throat. There's another sphincter at the bottom of your stomach. This one controls the food leaving the stomach and entering the small intestine.

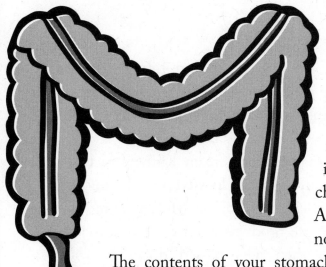

When the bolus lands in your stomach, your body gets to work breaking it down from something you'd recognize into chemical nutrients that your body uses for all its different functions. As your stomach muscles move the food around, acids split it apart and enzymes (proteins that cause chemical reactions) begin to break it down. After the stomach does its job, your food is now a mushy liquid.

The contents of your stomach then move on to the small intestine. This organ is only a little over an inch wide, which is why it's called the "small" intestine. However, it's about 20 feet long! In the small intestine, many enzymes come in from the nearby pancreas. These enzymes pummel the now-liquid food stuff, and are responsible for most of the digestion that takes place in the digestive system. Besides digesting, the small intestine absorbs the resulting nutrients into little fingers on its inner walls. The fingers are called villi, and they contain the tiny capillaries that receive the nutrients.

After your food has made its long journey through the small intestine, it's still mushy, but much of the liquid and nutrients have already been absorbed by your body. What's left now enters the large intestine. The large intestine is about three inches wide and around five feet long. It drapes around your abdominal cavity, running up one side, across the top, and down the other side. In the large intestine, more fluids are absorbed from what's left of the food, and "good" bacteria work on breaking down any tough food matter (like fiber or things like lettuce).

At this point, there's little liquid left, and anything that remains—stuff your body just can't use for anything—is a soft solid waste: poop (or if you're going to be fancy, "feces"). The last step for your now completely digested food is moving through your rectum. This is the end of your large intestine where feces travel before being expelled through your anus.

URINARY SYSTEM

Solid waste is handled through your large intestine and rectum. Liquid waste is also a problem because waste molecules are constantly produced by all the body's cells. These wastes enter your blood and are disposed of through the urinary system. One such waste product is called **urea**.

It's your kidneys' job to filter out urea from your bloodstream. Kidneys are bean shaped organs a bit bigger than a deck of cards. They're located near the middle of your back. Tiny kidney tubes filter and clean the blood while making our urine, which contains urea and all other waste products from the bloodstream.

The urine then gets passed down to your bladder through tubes called **ureters**. When the bladder is full your brain receives a message from nerves in the stretched bladder wall that tells you it's time to go to the bathroom.

WHAT'S IN IT FOR ME?

Now that you know how your body breaks down food, the next question is: Just how does it use what it has broken down?

Food is made of different kinds of nutrient molecules. When your digestive system breaks down food, it's reducing everything to its molecular level—first through saliva, then chewing, then each of the digestive organs. Along the way, your body pulls out the chemicals and molecules it needs and shuttles them off to be given to all of the cells all over your body.

WORDS TO KNOW

urea: waste product made from our cells.

ureters: tubes connecting the bladder to the kidneys.

NUTRIENT	WHAT IT DOES	FOUND IN
carbohydrates	main source of energy, easily used by the body	sugars
	for energy	bread, cereal, crackers
protein	cell growth and repair	meat
	makes hormones and enzymes	beans tofu
fats	provides back-up energy	dairy products
	provides insulation	sweets
vitamins	essential to body functioning	fruits
	helps immune system battles disease	vegetables
minerals	necessary for body functioning	vegetables beef liver

MAKE YOUR OWN TOOTH CAST

Using your teeth to chew is one of the first steps in the digestive process. You see them in the mirror when you brush, but have you ever really taken a good look at them? This project will let you see what your teeth look like from all angles, and how they fit together to make a good chewing surface.

SUPPLIES

- clay
- plastic wrap
- scissors
- construction paper
- tape
- plaster of Paris

IMPORTANT: Let a parent supervise this experiment, since you'll be putting stuff in your mouth.

1. Form the clay into two ½-inch thick wedges that you'll be able to fit in your mouth.

Carefully wrap each of the wedges in plastic wrap. This needs to be tight enough that it won't fall off, but loose enough that when you bite the wrap, your teeth won't puncture it.

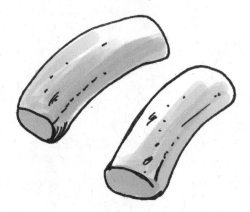

2. Bite into one of the wedges with your top teeth, making sure you get all the way back to your molars. Carefully pull it off your teeth and out of your mouth, then remove and discard the plastic. You should have a clear impression of your top set of teeth.

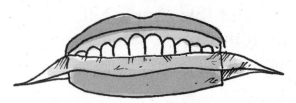

3. Repeat this with the bottom set of your teeth.

4. Cut the construction paper into two 2-inch strips.

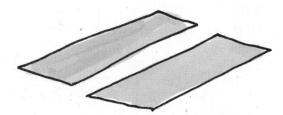

5. Wrap the paper around the top edge of both wedges. Make sure that at least an inch and a half of paper is above the edge of the clay. You'll be filling this with plaster of Paris, so it has to be high enough so that the plaster won't spill over.

6. Mix together some plaster of Paris in a paper cup with some water until you have a thick consistency, then pour it into your molds. Tap the clay on the table a little to be sure you don't have any air pockets.

7. Wait until the plaster is dry, then remove the paper and the clay. You'll have a perfect model of your teeth!

8. See if you can identify the different teeth and what you use them for in biting and chewing.

MAKE YOUR OWN NUTRITION BALANCE

If you look at the food pyramid created by the United States Department of Agriculture, you can figure out how much of each food group is recommended for your size and age. But sometimes it's hard to keep track of what you've eaten and from which food group. Here's an easy way to keep track by balancing dried beans. Once you build this simple balance, just move over beans from one side to the other. When the balance is even, you've eaten a balanced diet!

SUPPLIES

- wire coat hangers
- wire cutters
- pliers
- foam block
- string
- scissors
- small paper cups
- modeling clay
- beans
- paint in several colors

1. To make your balance, straighten out a coat hanger. Cut it about a foot long, so the hook is at one end. Use pliers to grip it better if you need to. This is the base of your balance.

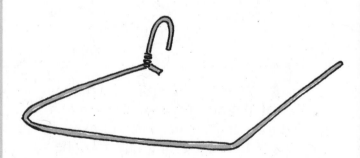

2. Stick the unhooked end of the coat hanger into the foam block. You've now assembled the stand.

3. Take another straight piece of coat hanger (about ten inches long). Bend each end into a hook, then tie four pieces of string (about four inches long each) to each end.

4. Poke four holes in one paper cup around the rims, then carefully tie one string into each hole. Repeat this with the second paper cup. These will be where you add and remove the counting beans.

5. Balance the free piece of coat hanger from the hook on your balance stand. You may have to slide it more to one side or the other until it's at the perfect spot to balance the empty cups. Once you've found the right spot, stick a small piece of modeling clay on either side of the balancing wire so it won't slide one way or the other. If you're still having problems balancing, you can also add a small piece of modeling clay as a weight to one side or the other.

continued on next page...

MAKE YOUR OWN
NUTRITION BALANCE continued

6. The balance is finished, so set it aside.

7. Count out 42 beans. Paint five beans orange, seven beans yellow, three beans blue, and six beans red (or choose your own colors, but keep the number of beans the same as listed here). You'll have 21 unpainted beans—these are your balance beans.

8. When the paint is dry, put all 42 beans in one cup. You're ready to start keeping track now.

9. Whenever you eat something during the day, move one of the beans to the second (currently empty) cup. Here's how to choose the beans:

If you eat:
- **a fruit or vegetable:** move an orange bean.
- **a grain:** move a yellow bean.
- **a dairy product:** move a blue bean.
- **a protein:** move a red bean.

10. If you've eaten a balanced diet during the day, your scale will be balanced and will let you know!

CHAPTER 4
MUSCLES

What moves the human body? Muscles, of course. Any movement you make at all—rolling your eyes at a bad joke, kicking the game-winning goal, even breathing while you sleep—it's all controlled by muscles. Your muscles are also hard at work moving parts of your body you can't even see.

Muscles move food through your digestive system, for example. They also make your heart beat and pump blood through your circulatory system.

When you think of a muscle, you might picture the bulge when you tighten your upper arm. But muscles actually come in all different shapes and sizes. They can be triangle shaped, like the one in your shoulder that helps you raise and lower your arm. They can be flat and wide, like abdominal muscles. And they can be ringed, like those controlling food coming in and out of your stomach.

When you're first born, you don't have much control over your movements. That's because babies have to train their brains to work together with their muscles. As you get older, you get much more control over your muscles. Some people, like athletes, dancers, or musicians, have such control over their muscles that they can perform amazing feats.

MUSCLE MAKE-UP

If you could see your muscles under your skin, they'd look like groups of slick bands. These bands are muscle fibers. These fibers are made up of thin threads called **fibrils**. And fibrils themselves are made of strands of protein. Binding the whole muscle together is a tough cover called a **sheath**.

Your brain sends messages to your muscles by sending signals along your nerves. When your muscle receives these signals from your brain, its fibers contract (a **contraction**). Whatever body part that particular muscle is attached to moves as well.

It's important to know that your muscles never push body parts—they only pull them. But they can move your body parts in a push-pull motion by working together.

DID YOU KNOW?

The smallest muscle and the smallest bone are found in the middle ear. The muscle is called the stapedius, and the bone is the stapes. They work together to help conduct sound vibrations through your ear so you can hear, and to protect against loud sounds.

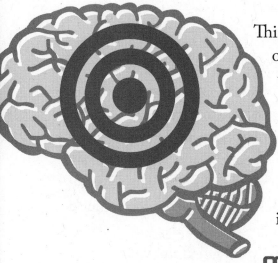

Think about throwing a ball. First, your biceps muscle on your upper arm *pulls* your forearm back to bring the ball up into throwing position. When you throw the ball forward, the muscle on the underside of your upper arm—your triceps—contracts, *pulling* your forearm down to complete the throw.

It's a little more complicated than you thought, isn't it?

MAKING THEM MOVE

You have different kinds of muscles, but they all work in pretty much the same way. Some of them are voluntary, meaning you choose to make them move—you decide to raise your hand or lift your foot to walk up a step. Other muscles are involuntary, meaning they move without you even thinking about it—like your heart muscle pumping blood or your stomach digesting food. But both kinds of movements are controlled by your brain. Your brain sends out signals through long nerve fibers, which then send the signals to your muscle fibers (by chemicals called neurotransmitters). This tells the muscle fibers just how to contract—how much, how often, and when. Now let's take a look at the kinds of voluntary and involuntary muscles.

DID YOU KNOW?

Olympic weightlifters train their muscles over many months and years in order to lift extreme amounts of weight above their heads. The most weight ever raised by an Olympic weightlifter was a humongous 586 pounds!

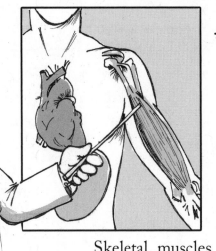

* **Skeletal.** Your skeletal muscles are the muscles that you have control over. With these, you can move your arms, legs, mouth, and eyes whenever you like. Their fibers are the longest and thickest of all. If you were to look at your skeletal muscles under a microscope, they'd look like striped rods.

Skeletal muscles are usually attached to your bones. They're attached with tough connective tissue bands called **tendons**. But not all skeletal muscles are connected to your bones. The skeletal muscles on your face, for example, are attached to your skin. This lets you make different facial expressions by moving things like your eyebrows and mouth.

Your skeletal muscles are strong, but they can get tired very quickly. If you squeeze your hand into a fist over and over again, you'll very quickly tire your hand. That's unlike your cardiac (heart) muscle, that pumps and pumps without getting tired.

DID YOU KNOW?

When your muscles cramp—causing hard, painful lumps—it's because they've contracted, and are staying that way. You need to gently stretch them to work them back out.

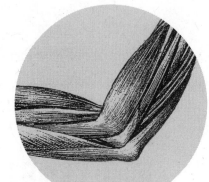

* **Smooth.** You don't choose to move your smooth muscles—they move on their own. Smooth muscle is in the walls of your blood vessels and air tubes, but also in the walls of your inner organs, such as your stomach, intestines, and bladder. For example, your stomach moves to pass food through it. You don't even have to think about it. In fact, it will happen even if you try with all your might to make it stop!

Smooth muscles do their job, day after day, without you giving them a second thought.

If you looked at your smooth muscles under a microscope, you'd see they're not striped or rods like skeletal muscles. Instead, they're pointed at the ends. They're bundled in flat sheets that look smooth. These muscles can stay contracted for long periods without tiring out, unlike your skeletal muscles.

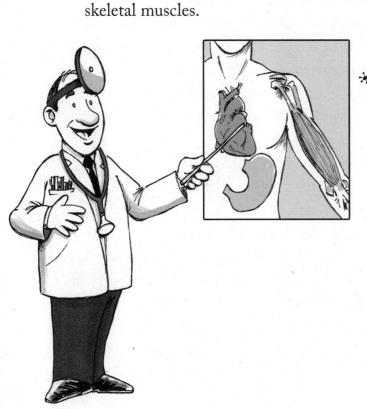

* **Cardiac.** As you can probably guess from the name, your cardiac muscles are the ones in the wall of your heart. Your cardiac muscle contracts constantly—it's what makes your heart beat. This is one muscle that never tires out. It just keeps on contracting and relaxing in a regular rhythm throughout your whole life. Under a microscope, your cardiac muscle cells look like striped, branched barrels.

MUSCLE MEMORY

When you learned how to walk, skip, throw a ball, or brush your teeth, you got better at it the more you did it. That's partly because your muscles were getting stronger as you grew. But it's also because of something called **muscle memory**.

As you repeat a movement over and over, your muscles begin to "remember" everything that happens. They remember exactly how hard to pull, when to stop pulling, and the angle they're pulling at. Of course, it's your brain and spinal cord learning how to control and coordinate groups of muscles.

That's why you don't hit yourself in the head with your hairbrush every morning when you try to brush your hair. Your arm, hand, and head all remember just where to position themselves so you end up with a good hair day—not a bad headache.

GROW, BABY, GROW!

If you've seen a person who works out all the time and pushes his or her muscles to the limit, you know that people can really grow huge muscles. When you exercise, you can increase the size of your muscles or make them firmer. But did you ever wonder what would happen if you just lay in bed all day, every day? If you did, your muscles would shrink, or **atrophy** (and you'd be really bored, too!).

Although the chance of you just hanging around, never lifting a single finger is pretty rare, it's still important to move your muscles and keep them strong. Muscles grow stronger when you exercise because every time you make your muscles work hard, some of the muscle fibers are damaged. (That's why your muscles ache if you do something you don't usually do, like lift something really heavy. The next day, your damaged muscle fibers are busy repairing.) When those fibers heal and regrow, the muscle becomes larger. When people work out really hard—lifting weights, for example—they intentionally damage their muscle fibers, then rest and let those fibers heal and build up. As they repeat the cycle, the fibers not only grow, but they increase in numbers as they split and form new fibers.

On the flip side, if someone doesn't use a muscle at all, it doesn't keep building new fibers, and the muscle will become smaller and weaker (atrophy). If you break your leg and have a cast on it all summer and don't run around, when the cast is removed those leg muscles may look smaller than on the other leg.

WORDS TO KNOW

muscle memory: the process of your muscles remembering how to work.
atrophy: when muscles get smaller and weaker.
sedentary: not moving around much.

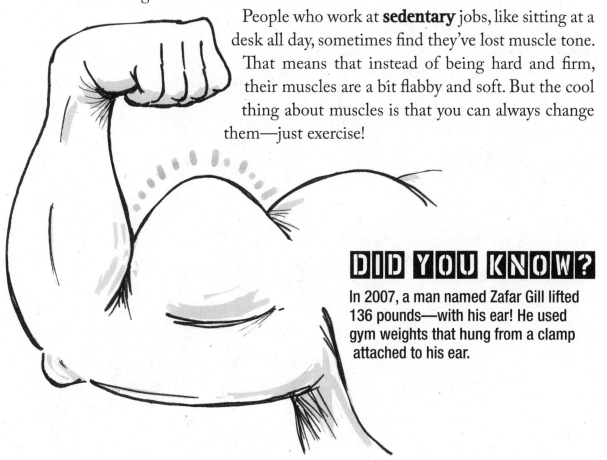

People who work at **sedentary** jobs, like sitting at a desk all day, sometimes find they've lost muscle tone. That means that instead of being hard and firm, their muscles are a bit flabby and soft. But the cool thing about muscles is that you can always change them—just exercise!

DID YOU KNOW?

In 2007, a man named Zafar Gill lifted 136 pounds—with his ear! He used gym weights that hung from a clamp attached to his ear.

TRY PLAYING WITH MUSCLE MEMORY

Although your muscles don't really have a brain of their own, your body tries very hard to learn your movements and perform them. This is especially true if it's a repetitive task like playing the piano or hitting a baseball. If you've ever felt like you knew how to do something so well you could practically do it in your sleep, that's thanks in part to muscle memory. Here's how to play a trick on your muscles and see muscle memory in action.

SUPPLIES

- a timer or clock with a second hand
- a narrow doorway (like in a closet)

1. If you have any bracelets or a watch on your wrist, take them off.

2. Stand in a narrow doorway, facing outward, with your hands hanging at your sides.

3. Press the backs of your wrists firmly against the doorframe. Time yourself for thirty seconds. Be sure you don't squirm around or else it won't work as well.

4. When the time is up, step out of the doorway and completely relax your arms, letting them hang limply next to your sides.

5. Look down at your arms. You may not be able to feel it, but your arms begin to "float" up all by themselves! (After just a couple of seconds, though, they'll respond normally again.) That's because your muscles are still trying to help you push hard against the doorway.

MAKE YOUR OWN WORKING MODEL HAND

1. Trace a parent's hand onto the craft foam (you can do your hand if you want, but a bigger hand is easier to work with). Cut it out. Be sure to angle the thumb almost at a right angle to your hand. This is because your thumb can move differently than your fingers.

2. Snip the straws into 3-inch sections. You'll need 14 pieces altogether.

3. Lay three pieces of straw onto one of the cutout hand's fingers, placing one for each segment of finger (between the knuckles). You don't want the pieces of straw to touch each other, so be sure to leave space right where the knuckle would be. Hot glue these into place.

4. Repeat with the remaining fingers. For the thumb, use two straw pieces (look at your thumb to figure out where to place them).

5. Cut four long pieces of straw, and line them up at the end of each of the fingers' straws. Again, leave a space between the last straw segment, so it will bend. Glue these into place.

SUPPLIES

- pencil
- craft foam
- scissors
- straws
- glue gun
- string

6. Cut five pieces of string, each long enough to run through each of the fingers, through the palm, and give you about four inches leftover. Thread one string through each finger's straws, and through the thumb's straws, too.

7. Glue (or tape) the string to the foam at the very tip of each finger.

8. When you gently pull the strings, the fingers will move just like in your real hand!

45

CHAPTER 5
BONES

If you pick up an earthworm and hold it by one end, what happens? It slumps right over and curls down along your fingers. Why? Because it doesn't have bones. There's no framework inside that holds it up, like your skeleton does for you. Without your skeleton, you too would be a slug-like mass of muscles and organs. You'd probably be able to move around (like the earthworm), but you wouldn't be able to stand upright and do all the things you're used to doing—like running and jumping.

But the bones of your skeleton do a lot more than let you stand up and move around. They also make your blood cells and protect your organs from damage.

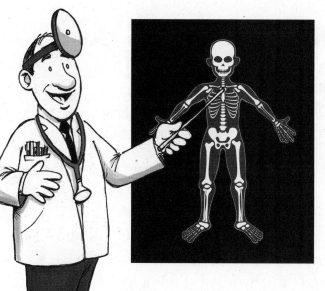

Scientists divide the human skeleton into two parts. The first part is called the **axial skeleton**. It is centered around the midline (axis) of the body and consists of your backbone, **sternum**, ribs, and skull. The axial skeleton protects organs like your lungs, heart, and brain.

The second part of the human skeleton is called the **appendicular skeleton**. These are the bones in your limbs, like your arm and leg bones. This skeleton lets you move around and do everything from running and jumping to opening a jar of pickles.

WORDS TO KNOW

axial skeleton: the ribs, backbone, skull, and sternum.

sternum: the wide, flat bone that joins your ribs together in front, also called the breastbone.

appendicular skeleton: arm and leg bones.

periosteum: the membrane on the outside of a bone.

compact bone: the white, hard, outer part of bones.

bone marrow: the middle of the bone, which is soft and fatty.

BONE CONSTRUCTION

When people die, the soft parts of their body decay. The only thing left behind is their bones. That's why the symbol for pirates or deadly chemicals is the skull and crossbones. But why do bones stick around so much longer than other body parts? It's because of what they're made of.

Bones have to be lightweight (so we can move around easily) but very strong. An adult's bones make up only 15 percent of their body weight, but ounce for ounce, they're stronger than steel! This means that if you had the same amount of bone as steel, your bones would be stronger.

Your bones have layers. The outer membrane is a very thin but tough layer called the **periosteum**. The periosteum has blood vessels running through it that allow blood to enter the bone.

The next layer is the **compact bone**. This is the hard, white stuff you think of when you imagine skeletons. But if your skeleton were made completely of compact bone, it would be too heavy. But it's not too heavy because underneath the compact bone is a kind of network of thin pieces of bone. This is sometimes called "spongy bone" because of the way it looks.

Bones have another part inside, a soft tissue called **bone marrow.** And inside the bone marrow are special cells called stem cells. These cells give rise to all our blood cells.

DID YOU KNOW?

Infants have more bones in their bodies than adults. That's because some of a baby's bones are still "knitting" together, making several bones into one.

WORDS TO KNOW

cartilage: stiff, flexible tissue that mostly converts to bone in adults.

ossification: the process of bone formation with the help of minerals like calcium.

NOT QUITE BONE

Your ears and nose aren't made of bone. They're made of **cartilage**, a tough connective tissue. When babies are developing in their mom's womb, most of their bones are made out of cartilage. As they grow, the cartilage turns into hard bones. This process is called **ossification**. But there's still plenty of cartilage (besides your nose and ears). Cartilage covers the ends of your bones at the movable joints, rib cartilages connect your ribs to your breastbone, and the rings in the wall of your trachea are made of cartilage.

JOINTS: WHERE BONES COME TO MEET EACH OTHER

The place where your bones come together is called a joint. Joints help you move. The kind of movement you're capable of doing at a joint depends on the kind of joint that's there. There are different kinds of joints, each performing differently than the others.

* **Ball and socket.** Examples of this are the joints that connect your arm to your shoulder, and your leg to your hip. The bone of your arm or leg ends in a knob, or ball, that fits into the bowl-shaped socket of your shoulder or hip. This setup lets you rotate your arm or leg in all different directions.

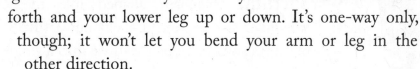

Humerus and scapula as a ball and socket.

* **Hinge.** This kind of joint can be found at your elbows and knees. A hinge joint is similar to the hinge on a door. It lets you move your lower arm back and forth and your lower leg up or down. It's one-way only, though; it won't let you bend your arm or leg in the other direction.

* **Saddle.** Where your thumb bone meets your hand bone is called a saddle joint. Picture a saddle, right-side up. Then picture a second saddle, upside down. If you laid the upside-down saddle on top of the first one, you'd get a saddle joint. This kind of joint allows you to move your thumb forward, backward, and side to side so you can grab on to things. It's not quite as flexible as the ball and socket joint, though.

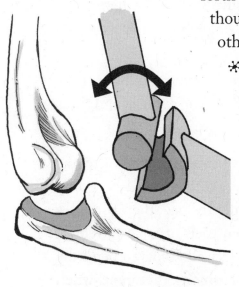

Humerus and ulna as a hinge.

* **Pivot.** The backbone in your neck is an example of a pivot joint. This lets your head move from side to side smoothly.

STANDING UP STRAIGHT

Your backbone, or spine, is actually a chain of bones called **vertebrae**. Each vertebra looks slightly oval on the bottom with three "wings" behind. It also has a hole in the arch. This is where your spinal cord, the nerve cord that extends from your brain, runs. Your vertebrae protect your spinal cord and support your weight.

The vertebrae are divided into groups:

* **Cervical vertebrae.** These are the first seven bones in your spinal column. They are in your neck and they support your head.

* **Thoracic vertebrae.** These are the next twelve vertebrae in your backbone. They're larger than cervical vertebrae, and each is connected to a rib.

* **Lumbar vertebrae.** The five lumbar vertebrae come next and are in your lower back. They're the largest of the vertebrae because their job is to support the weight of your body.

* **Sacrum.** This isn't shaped like the other vertebrae; it's triangular shaped, and it starts out as five vertebrae when you're born. As you get older, they fuse into a single bone. The sacrum is part of your pelvis.

* **Coccyx.** The last part of your backbone is the coccyx, or tailbone. Like the sacrum, this starts out as several bones when you're born, and fuses into one when you grow older.

Your spine is flexible because the vertebrae aren't fused to one another. You'd be pretty stiff if that were true! Instead, there are discs of cartilage between each of your vertebrae. This cartilage not only allows us to bend the spine, but it also cushions the spine when you're doing something really active, like running or jumping.

WORDS TO KNOW

vertebrae: the bones that make up the spinal column.

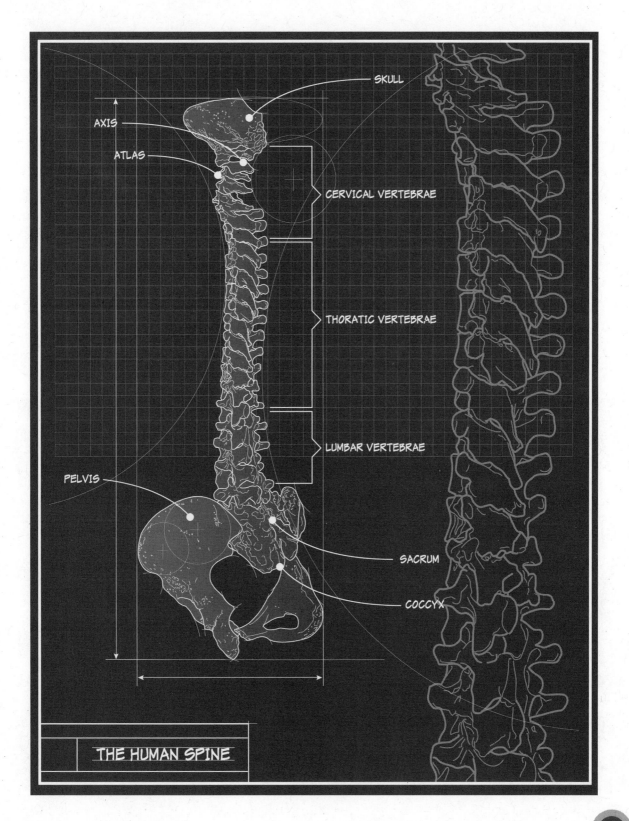

SKULL

AXIS

ATLAS

CERVICAL VERTEBRAE

THORATIC VERTEBRAE

LUMBAR VERTEBRAE

PELVIS

SACRUM

COCCYX

THE HUMAN SPINE

SHAPES AND SIZES OF BONES

When you think of bones, the first shape that may come to mind is a long bone with knobby ends. Some bones do actually look that way, of course. The long bones of your legs and arms look just like that. But other bones have different shapes, like your skull, for instance. It's made of several plates that join together. And your two pelvic bones are wide and slightly **concave**, much different than the shape of any other bones in your body. There's a big range in size, too. Your femur, or thigh bone, is the largest. The smallest? The three tiny bones inside your inner ear.

WORDS TO KNOW

concave: curving inward.
enamel: the protective outside layer on teeth.

STRONG CHOMPERS

As strong as your bones are, your teeth are even stronger! That's because they're covered with something called **enamel**, the hardest stuff in the human body. But it's not indestructible, of course. Its weakness is sugar decay. The sugars and natural bacteria in your mouth can team up to break down the enamel. So brush those teeth well!

Underneath the enamel is a yellow bone-like material called dentin. If you have a cavity, it's usually a hole in the enamel that leaves the dentin exposed. At the center of your teeth is pulp. Pulp is the soft innards of your tooth. It contains important blood vessels and nerves. Its nerves are the tooth's main message carriers to the brain. The part of your teeth that's visible is called the crown. Your teeth are connected to your jaws by their roots. These are covered by a bony substance called cementum. Softer than dentin, cementum anchors fibers that hold the tooth in its socket.

THE LEG BONE'S CONNECTED TO THE KNEE BONE . . .

If your bones were fastened firmly together, you wouldn't be able to bend, twist, or move the way you do. But your bones can't just be floating around inside your skin, either. The answer is that bones are attached to each other by **ligaments**.

Ligaments are elastic, fibrous structures. Since they're elastic, they can stretch slightly. That's why you stretch out before playing sports or exercising. You're making your body more flexible by stretching out the ligaments in preparation for action.

BREAK TIME

Imagine running with your friends, playing soccer, when an opponent running the other way kicks for the ball, misses—and gets your leg instead. Crack! You hear a loud noise and you're on the ground, grabbing your leg in pain. The news isn't great: You've got a broken bone.

Although bones are pretty strong, sometimes accidents happen and you end up with a broken bone, called a **fracture**. Any of your bones can break—from your fingers to your toes. If you've got a break, the doctor will take an x-ray to see what's broken and how badly. Not every break is the same. There are different ways that bones can break.

WORDS TO KNOW

ligaments: elastic tissue that attaches bones to each other.

fracture: another name for a broken bone.

lamellar bone: a strong, hard type of bone material.

There are different types of fractures:

* **Spiral fracture:** when the bone is broken because it's been twisted and there are several breaks.

* **Oblique fracture:** a break that is diagonal across the length of your bone.

* **Transverse fracture:** a break that's at a right angle to the length of your bone.

* **Compound fracture:** when the bone is broken and it pokes through the skin.

If a bone is broken, the doctor will line up the broken parts of the bone the right way, and then a cast will be put around the injured body part to keep it from moving around. This way, the bones will stay properly aligned and won't wiggle out of place while the healing process begins.

The broken bone and the tissue that's around it will bleed and then start to clot (like you read about in the chapter on blood). After a couple of days, your blood will carry a component that will lay down a "mesh" of fibers. These fibers criss-cross each other and "weave" into new bone material. Your cast may come off at this point, although this kind of bone isn't as hard as your old bone. Harder bone called **lamellar bone** eventually grows over the woven bone, and then you're practically good as new.

Generally, the younger you are, the faster your bones will heal. You can help the process along by eating foods that are high in calcium, the mineral that makes our bones hard (try foods like dairy products, cabbage, or orange juice).

YOUR HEART'S CAGE

You can feel your ribs if you press on the side of your chest—the hard, bumpy bones under your skin. The pairs of ribs start at your backbone, curve around your body to protect your chest's organs, and meet in the front, at the sternum (breastbone). This grouping of ribs is called your rib cage, and it does a great job of protecting your heart and lungs.

MAKE YOUR OWN DECALCIFYING BONE EXPERIMENT

One of the things that make bones strong are the minerals inside it. Here's how to remove those minerals and end up with a much different bone.

Note: Adult supervision is needed.

1. Put the bone in the bowl.

SUPPLIES

- chicken bone (get a long bone from a leg if you can)
- hydrochloric acid (from the pharmacy)
- very large glass bowl
- rubber gloves
- water
- baking soda

2. Ask an adult to pour the hydrochloric acid over the bone, completely covering it.

3. The next morning, fill another bowl with one cup of water and two tablespoons of baking soda. Dump out the hydrochloric acid from the first bowl and, wearing the rubber gloves, pick up the bone. Put it in the water and baking soda solution. This will neutralize the acid that's left on the bone.

4. After your bone has soaked in the second mixture for about ten minutes, take it out. Do you see the difference? Without the minerals making it hard—it's as floppy as rubber! If you have a very long bone, you can even try to tie a knot in it.

MAKE YOUR OWN JOINTS

It's amazing how your joints come together and function the way they do. In fact, carpenters mimic the human body's joints when they assemble things like door hinges. Here's how to make model joints so you can really see how the bones move together to help your body's mobility.

1. For each joint, you'll need to use two blocks. Draw the joint parts onto the blocks, then cut them out with the craft file (see diagrams for pictures of joints). When you're finished, assemble your joints to see how smoothly the parts go together.

2. Ball and socket joint: cut a gentle "scoop" out of a square piece of foam. This is the socket part of the joint. From another piece of foam, cut a straight piece that has a knob on the end. This is the ball that fits into the socket. You've got ball and socket joints on your hips and shoulders.

3. Saddle joint: Take two pieces of foam about the same size. Round the top edges of each so they are the shape of a mailbox. From each, scoop out a saddle shape in the middle. Then flip one upside down, turn it 90 degrees, and let it rest inside the first saddle. This is like the joint for your thumb. Try moving the top saddle left and right, and then the bottom one left and right. You've got quite a bit of mobility in your thumb, but you can see how it stops at a certain point (like if you were doing a hitchhiker motion) because of the lip of the second saddle.

4. Pivot joint: Cut one piece of foam into a circle with the middle missing (like a donut), and a second piece into a ball. Rest the circle on top of the ball. This is like a joint in your neck—it can move in a full turning radius. Your ligaments, muscles, tendons, and skin stop it from spinning around out of control, though!

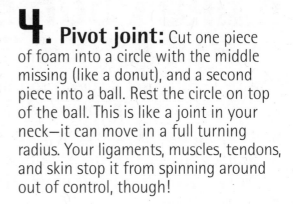

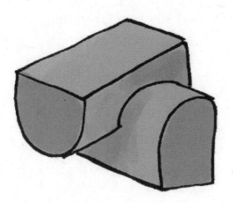

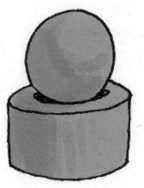

5. Hinge joint: It's hard to make a hinge joint out of foam, but it's easy to spot one—just look at any door. This is like your elbow or knee. You can see how it easily moves open and closed in one direction—but it's not able to continue in a full, 360-degree motion.

MAKE YOUR OWN FLEXIBLE SPINE

You probably don't spend too much time thinking about your spine, but it's really pretty amazing. Not only does it house your spinal cord, sending signals all over your body, but it helps your entire body stay upright. Even though it's stiff, it's also surprisingly flexible. Here's how to explore your flexible spine.

SUPPLIES

- spools of thread (they don't have to be empty)
- string
- large marshmallows

1. String the spools of thread together. Knot both ends. It's important that you make sure the string doesn't have a lot of extra room. Tie the knots so the spools are very snug together.

2. This represents your spine without any cushioning between the vertebrae. Try bending this spine and moving it as you would your back. It's pretty hard to do it.

3. Take the inflexible spine apart.

4. Cut the marshmallows in half. Then, string all the spools of thread together again—but this time, string the marshmallows in between each spool. You may have to poke a small hole in the center of the marshmallow to get the string through (if it gets too sticky, just dust the cut end of the marshmallow with powdered sugar). Tie off the ends as before.

5. Now you've got a different kind of spine—a flexible one. See how that extra "padding" between the vertebrae helps make it move more easily?

CHAPTER 6
CELLS

You've seen how your lungs bring oxygen into your body so your cells can use it for energy. And you've seen how blood cells move around your body. But what is a cell?

Cells are the smallest living things in your body. They're sometimes called the body's "building blocks." Scientists aren't sure how many cells are in your body, but estimates range between 50 to 100 *trillion*! And keep in mind that the number of cells in your body changes constantly, as old cells die and new ones are created.

WORDS TO KNOW

cell membrane: the cell's thin outer boundary.

cytoplasm: the jelly that fills the cell.

nucleus: the part of the cell that holds your genetic information.

organelles: the tiny parts of a cell.

All living creatures have cells. Plant cells are a bit different than human and animal cells. But our cells have the same basic job—to maintain the human body and care for it at a cellular level. Non-living things don't have cells—you're not going to find a cell in a rock or your shoe.

Cells work hard to get energy from food, fuel other cells, clean up other dead cells, gobble up invading germs, and even reproduce themselves. They're pretty busy, bustling around inside of you like a microscopic city hard at work every day.

YOUR CELLS: A CLOSE-UP LOOK

If you want to look at a cell from your body, you'll need a microscope. The first thing you might notice about your cell is that it has a border around it. That's the **cell membrane**. It holds everything inside the cell.

But your cell membrane is not quite solid. Materials can move in and out—but only if the guards let them through. That's right; your cell membrane contains proteins that act as guards. If something belongs in the cell, the guard proteins let it enter.

The cell itself is filled with a gooey, jelly-like substance called **cytoplasm** and also a central area called the **nucleus**. What is the stuff inside the cell? Well, just like your body has organs—your heart and stomach, for example—your cells have tiny parts that function as their "organs." They are called **organelles** (their name means "tiny organs").

DID YOU KNOW?

Cells got their name because, under a microscope, they look like little rooms, or "cells."

MOM, IS THAT YOU?

Cells can make copies of themselves. The copies are called "daughter" cells. Each daughter cell is an exact replica of the original "mother" cell. The process of a cell dividing to reproduce is called **mitosis**. Without mitosis, you wouldn't be able to create all the new cells your body needs when the old ones wear out.

Some organelles are:

* **Nucleus.** Inside each cell is a nucleus, the control center that contains all the **genetic** information about you. This info is contained in microscopic strands of material called **deoxyribonucleic acid (DNA)**, and **ribonucleic acid (RNA)**.

* **Mitochondria.** Sometimes called the "mighty mitochondria," these submarine-shaped organelles are the power houses that produce most of the energy your cells need to live and perform their functions.

* **Endoplasmic reticulum.** This tongue-twister name is appropriate for this organelle—it's shaped like a stack of envelopes. Their job is to make proteins.

* **Golgi apparatus.** The Golgi apparatus—which looks like a stack of bent pancakes—packages up the proteins and sends them to the cell membrane so the proteins pass out to the environment outside that cell, to be used as your body needs them.

* **Ribosomes.** Tiny little spheres called ribosomes make protein.

WORDS TO KNOW

mitosis: how a cell splits up.
genetic: related to the origin of something; things about you that are passed from parent to child.
deoxyribonucleic acid (DNA): the substance that carries your genetic information, the "blueprint" of who you are.
ribonucleic acid (RNA): similar to DNA, RNA helps make proteins in your body.

* **Lysosomes.** These organelles are responsible for the cell clean-up. Armed with enzymes, they break down old organelles or invading germs to get rid of them from the cell.

SPECIAL JOBS, SPECIAL CELLS

There are more than 200 different kinds of cells in your body! Each kind has a specific job to do, so it might need a special shape or feature in order to do that job effectively. Some examples of different types of cells are:

* **Blood cells.** You've seen that you have red and white blood cells and platelets, all performing different jobs in your blood stream.

* **Melanin cells.** These cells are in your skin, and they're responsible for producing skin color that protects the skin from damaging rays in sunlight.

* **Muscle cells.** These are long cells, and they contract forcefully, usually to cause movement.

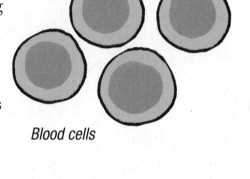

Blood cells

Muscle cells

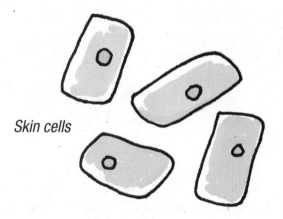

Skin cells

* **Skin cells.** Cells called epithelial cells are layered to form the outside layer of your skin. We'll learn more about skin cells in the next chapter.

MAKE YOUR OWN EDIBLE CELL

1. Pour powdered gelatin into a large bowl.

2. Stir in boiling water. Be sure to mix it at least three minutes to make certain the gelatin is completely dissolved.

3. Spray a plastic cup with nonstick cooking spray, then fill it halfway with gelatin. Put it in the refrigerator to chill.

4. When it's firm, take your cup out of the fridge. Put a gumball in the center of the gelatin (to represent the cell's nucleus). Then, use the candy to make the rest of the organelles in the cell: round cake sprinkles (ribosomes), red fruit leather (endoplasmic reticulum), green fruit leather (Golgi bodies), and hot tamales (mitochondria).

5. Make another batch of gelatin, and while it's still liquid, pour it very slowly into the cup. If you pour down the side of the cup, you'll get better results.

SUPPLIES

- two 8-ounce packages of lemon powdered gelatin (or another pale color)
- large bowl
- 2½ cups boiling water
- nonstick cooking spray
- plastic cup
- assorted candies like fruit leather, round cake sprinkles, gumballs, hot tamales

6. Carefully return the cup to the refrigerator until it's firm.

7. When it's ready, carefully slide the cell out of the cup. If you're having trouble, you can try sliding a butter knife around the edges. Or, if it's a disposable cup, just peel it away.

8. Examine your cell before eating—you should be able to see all the organelles inside!

CHAPTER 7
SKIN

What keeps everything inside you from spilling out? It's your skin, of course. Your skin is the part of you that people see, it's the boundaries of your physical self, and it also happens to be the largest organ in your body.

That's right—your skin is an organ, like your heart, stomach, and liver. Your skin grows with you, and performs important tasks for your body. It protects your innards from infection and injuries, helps keep you cool or warm, and makes vitamin D.

Most of your skin is about a tenth of an inch thick, except around areas like your heels, where it's thicker, and under your eyes, where it's thinner. Even as thin as it is, it's made of two layers, the **epidermis** and the **dermis**.

EPIDERMIS

The epidermis is the water-resistant outer layer of your skin—the surface of your skin. It is a sheet made of many cells crowded together.

New cells are always being made near the bottom of the epidermis layer. As they move upward, forcing the older cells upward as well, they get more and more flattened. They fill with a tough protein called keratin and then they die, so the top part of the epidermis is made of many flat, dead, cell husks. This keratinized layer is a tough skin barrier that protects you against the outside world.

Eventually, the oldest of the dead cells—the ones on the very top layer—fall off. You lose these dead skin cells constantly, even when you're asleep. You actually lose around 40,000 skin cells every minute! But new ones keep getting created and moving upward to replace them.

WORDS TO KNOW

epidermis: the outer layer of the skin.

dermis: the thick layer of the skin below the epidermis.

sebum: the oily secretion of the sebaceous glands. With perspiration it moistens and protects the skin.

DERMIS

Beneath the epidermis is the dermis layer. Unlike the epidermis, the dermis is a connective tissue, meaning its cells are separated form one another by a jelly that contains lots of strong fibers. The dermis contains the skin's sweat glands, blood vessels, hair follicles, and nerve endings. Many of these nerve endings go up into the epidermis as well, so both the dermis and epidermis let you feel heat, cold, and touch because of their nerve endings.

Skin

65

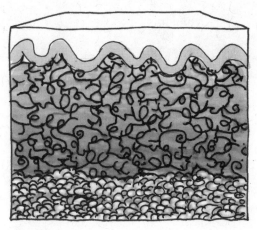

Dermis

Sweat glands are tiny tubes that begin down in your dermis and go right through to your epidermis. This is where the sweat—mostly water with a little salt—is released on the surface of your skin and reduces body heat and helps keep you cool.

Connected to your hair follicles are small glands called sebaceous glands. These secrete an oily substance called **sebum**. The sebum helps keep your skin supple, so it does not dry or crack. It may also help to make your skin water-resistant. Did you think your skin was waterproof? No, it isn't, but it can resist it for some time. When you take a shower, for example. But when you finally come out of the pool after swimming all day, your skin is wrinkled. That's because the sebum has washed away after lengthy exposure to the water. The water was able to get in and saturate the skin, making it wrinkled.

BRRR!

When you're cold, your skin has a bad time. Your body needs to keep its deeper organs warm, so it sends more hot blood there, and less of it out to the skin, which gets cold. And what's more, remember those hair follicles? Attached to each follicle is a tiny muscle. When you're cold, those muscles contract, raising the hair follicles all over your body—making goosebumps! It could be that your body is trying to raise hair to keep you warm, like an animal's fur. But you also start shivering—your muscles begin contracting and relaxing quickly. The contracting muscles generate heat, warming you up.

SKIN, HEAL THYSELF

We've seen how platelets in your blood close up wounds by clotting the blood and forming scabs. But what happens if it's a more serious injury, like a large or deep cut, or a bad burn? Your skin heals these, too, although sometimes you need help from a doctor. But then it's up to your body to heal that damage to your skin.

When your skin heals a more serious injury, it forms scar tissue at the wound. Scar tissue is a little different from normal skin. It doesn't have hair follicles or sweat glands. It also makes the skin look different from normal, so you'll see a "scar" even after the healing is done.

Scarred skin is usually thicker and paler than normal skin. It also doesn't move as easily as regular skin does. It's a little "tighter." Scarred skin is also more sensitive to sunlight.

DID YOU KNOW?

Your fingerprints developed when you were still a baby, growing inside your mom!

FINGERPRINTS

Your fingertips have tiny raised ridges on them. These are called friction ridges. You know them as your fingerprints, and they're not only different from finger to finger, but also different from anyone else's. Nobody in the world has the same fingerprints you do.

Your fingerprints may all look the same to you, but there are actually different types of patterns in them. These patterns are called loops, whorls, and arches. If one of your loops leans to the left, it's a left loop. Same goes for a right-leaning loop. There are also tented arches, double loop whorls, and other variations.

HAIR

Hair follicles are the parts of your skin where hair grows. Although the first place you think of hair growing is on your head, you've actually got tiny hairs all over your body.

In fact, you've got hair everywhere except the palms of your hands, eyelids, lips, and on the bottoms of your feet.

Hair is alive only at the root, where it's inside your skin. As it grows, the cells form keratin (a protein). Then, as your hair continues to grow, the cells push out the dead cells and continue growing and pushing, growing and pushing—and you see your hair grow. Even though the hair on your head is made of dead cells, it can still look good because of the sebum oil that coats each strand as it grows.

Your body hair protects your innards from dust and bacteria—like when your nose hair catches airborne debris and stops it from entering your body.

NAILS

Although you may think your nails aren't as impressive as a grizzly's giant claws, your nails are pretty tough and hard, and they help protect the tips of your fingers and toes. You may not use your nails to rip apart logs or catch salmon like the grizzly, but you can use them to scratch an itch, strum a guitar, or peel an orange. Like your hair, the main part of the nail that you see is made of dead cells that keep getting pushed out farther as the living part of the nail grows.

KERATIN

FROSTBITE

When it is deathly cold out (below freezing, 32 degrees Fahrenheit) the blood vessels in your fingers and toes will contract to preserve warmth. When this happens, the flow of blood to your fingers and toes is restricted, and because less blood is able to flow to your fingers and toes, they lose their warmth over time and freeze. When this happens, the skin can begin to discolor, turning purple or black and blisters can occur. If it gets bad enough, wounds can open on your skin and you will not be able to feel them. Then, disease can set in and you could lose your fingers, toes, or other parts of your body.

MAKE YOUR OWN HOMEMADE SKIN CARE PRODUCTS

Your skin needs to replace its moisture to stay soft and healthy. But there's no reason to rely on pharmaceuticals and manufactured chemicals to do the job—you can use some natural food items instead. Here's how to make your own skin care products to help your skin maintain its good health.

EASY SKIN SCRUB

1. Fill the glass jar partway with some of the sugar and set aside.

2. Split each vanilla bean carefully lengthwise. Be careful not to cut all the way through. You're trying to split it open to reveal the seeds inside. Flatten it out and cut it into pieces.

3. Layer the rest of the sugar and vanilla bean pieces in the jar, cover it tightly, and set it aside for a few weeks. Make sure it's in a dry place so the sugar doesn't clump.

4. When it's ready, sift through and pick out any vanilla chunks.

5. To use your scrub, mix a little bit of water with the scented sugar and gently rub it into your skin. Rinse well and enjoy your smooth skin.

SUPPLIES

- glass jar with cover
- 1 cup granulated sugar
- 2 vanilla beans
- knife

STRAWBERRY FIELD MASK

SUPPLIES

- 1 tablespoon plain yogurt
- bowl
- ½ cup strawberries
- fork

1. Put the yogurt into a bowl. Set aside.

2. Mash up the strawberries with the fork, then mix them into the yogurt. (It's okay to sneak a bite or two!)

3. Spread the mix over your face and let it sit for 20 minutes to deep clean your skin. When the time's up, rinse well and pat your skin dry.

BUBBLE BATH

SUPPLIES

- 1 egg white
- 1 tablespoon honey
- ½ cup gentle liquid soap like Ivory

1. Carefully mix everything together. Be careful not to be too vigorous, or else it will all start foaming!

2. Pour the mix under running water as you're filling the bathtub.

BATH FIZZIES

1. Mix together the cornstarch, citric acid powder, and baking soda.

2. Add in the canola oil and mix really well. Add food coloring and essential oil if you're using them. You'll end up with a soft dough that feels a little crumbly.

3. Shape the fizzies into small balls, or press them into molds if you have them.

4. Let the fizzies sit for 48 hours. When you're ready to use one, drop it into a warm bath and watch it explode into bubbles.

MAKE YOUR OWN FINGERPRINT KIT

Like a detective, you can "lift" fingerprints from around your home with this fingerprint kit. Skin has oils in it, and when you touch something it leaves an invisible mark shaped like your fingerprint. Use this kit to lift fingerprints from your piggy bank and find out just who's been checking out your funds!

SUPPLIES

- graphite pencils
- sandpaper
- white piece of paper
- small container

- duster (you can use an old make-up brush or even a feather duster)
- clear tape
- magnifying glass

1. Sharpen the pencils really well to get started. Hold a pencil and sandpaper over a piece of white paper. Begin rubbing the tip of the pencil on the sandpaper vigorously. You'll start shaving down the pencil into a dust that falls onto the paper. (Be careful not to inhale any of this dust!)

2. When you've got a good pile of graphite, carefully pick up the paper, roll up two sides gently, and pour your fingerprinting dust into the container. You're ready to hunt for fingerprints!

3. To test your kit, press your finger firmly and evenly on a mirror or glass (a flat surface is ideal).

4. Gently dip the top of your duster into the fingerprinting dust, and carefully brush it over the print you made. It helps to spin the brush a little bit as you move it over the print. You should be able to make out the print clearly.

5. Take a piece of clear tape and firmly smooth it over the print. Then, slowly peel back the tape. You've "lifted" a print onto the tape!

6. You can now mount the tape on a white sheet of paper and look at it closely under a magnifying glass. Look for the different patterns made by the ridges.

7. You can even print everyone in your house (let them press right on the piece of tape, dust it lightly so you can see it, and mount it on paper). Then, you'll have a record of everyone's prints!

CHAPTER 8
BRAIN

There sure are a lot of things going on in your body, aren't there? Who's in charge of all this activity? Your brain, of course. Your brain is the lead organ in your **nervous system**, just like your heart is the leading organ in your circulatory system.

Your nervous system carries messages from your brain to all the parts of your body, telling them what to do. Along with the brain, the most important part of your nervous system is your spinal cord. This nerve cord travels down through (and is protected by) the vertebrae in your spinal column. The brain and the spinal cord together are called the central nervous system.

Your central nervous system contains billions of nerve cells called neurons. Neurons have both long arms and short arms. It looks like a spikey spider. The long arms are called axons and the shorter ones are called dendrites. The dendrites receive messages. The axons send messages.

What exactly are these messages and how are they passed along? They are electrical signals that travel along the cell membrane of the nerve cell. The fastest message, called an impulse, races along the axon. This signal then jumps along a small gap to the next nerve cell in line, and to the next, like a chain reaction.

But not all nerve cells are alike—some are **sensory cells**. Their job is to carry

WORDS TO KNOW

nervous system: the parts of the body that receive and interpret stimuli and send responses.

sensory cells: cells that carry messages from your sense organs to your brain.

motor cells: cells that carry messages from your brain to your muscles.

information from your sense organs, like your nose or your tongue. There are also **motor cells**. These cells pass messages from your brain and spinal cord to your muscles, telling them to pick up your fork, run, or clap your hands.

CONTROL CENTRAL

The human brain is divided into three main parts: the cerebrum, the cerebellum, and the brain stem. Each part is in charge of a very important group of tasks.

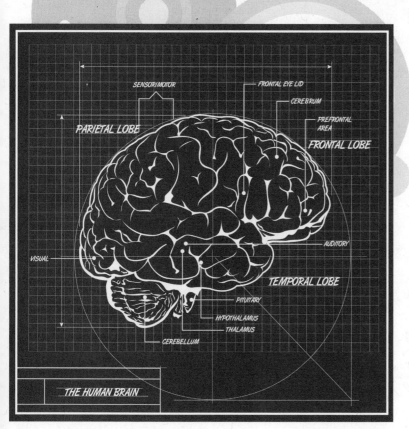

SENSORIMOTOR
FRONTAL EYE LID
CEREBRUM
PARIETAL LOBE
PREFRONTAL AREA
FRONTAL LOBE
AUDITORY
VISUAL
TEMPORAL LOBE
PITUITARY
HYPOTHALAMUS
THALAMUS
CEREBELLUM

THE HUMAN BRAIN

✳ **The Cerebrum.** Your cerebrum is divided into two halves, the left and right half (called hemispheres). This is the biggest part of your brain and is responsible for your thinking, knowing, and remembering. It also lets you be aware of everything you sense and controls your voluntary movements. The left cerebral hemisphere controls the right side of your body, and the right cerebral hemisphere controls the left side of your body.

LOBE	WHAT IT DOES	HOW YOU USE IT
frontal	controls impulses and judgement	you can choose not to touch a red-hot coal with your bare hands
	language, problem solving, emotions, and socialization	you decide if you should talk to the new kid in school
parietal	interprets your senses	you can feel that the cat is soft or the splinter is painful
	interprets numbers, letters, and words	you can read or do math
temporal	interprets what you hear	you know your mom's calling you for dinner
	memory	you remember what you had for dinner last night
occiptal	seeing	you see the dinner on your plate is leftovers

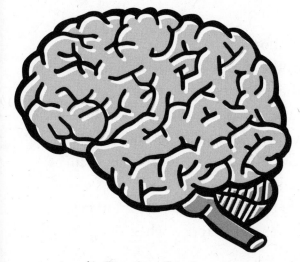

✱ **The Cerebellum.** The name cerebellum means "little brain" in Latin. That's just what this part of your brain looks like—a small replica of your cerebrum. But your cerebellum is important for making your movements smooth and coordinated. It's what helps you walk smoothly, catch a ball, do a handstand, perform the backstroke, or even stand without falling over.

✱ **Brain Stem.** Your brain stem is the smallest part of your brain and it continues downward, to the spinal cord. It's the part of your brain that controls the basic life functions, like your heartbeat, breathing, swallowing, and blood pressure. Just above the brain stem is a small part of the brain called the hypothalamus. This controls your body temperature, digestion, hunger, growth, and emotions like anger.

THE MYSTERY OF YOUR MIND

Your brain is an incredible organ. In fact, scientists haven't yet unlocked many of its mysteries.

One of the most interesting parts of your brain can't be seen. It's your mind. What is your mind? Nobody really knows. It's impossible to define. Your brain is a physical thing, but your mind isn't. Everybody has the same general brain structure, but your mind is unlike any other mind. The mind is a combination of your thoughts, experiences, feelings, intelligence, emotions, memory, imagination, sense of humor—it is who you are as a person. But where, exactly, is your mind?

DID YOU KNOW?

An adult human's brain weighs about 3 pounds, but a sperm whale's brain weighs 17 pounds—the biggest brain in nature!

Some scientists and philosophers think the mind is totally separate from the brain. Others think that without the brain, the mind cannot exist. What do you think? People who have suffered brain injuries often struggle with basic brain and memory functions. You've seen how different parts of your brain help you move, think, talk, hear, and do everything else you do during the day. But what if one part of your brain gets injured? Here are some of the symptoms that happen when one part of someone's brain is hurt:

SYMPTOM	PART OF BRAIN AFFECTED
Very uncoordinated when walking or reaching out to touch things	Cerebellum
Slurred speech	Cerebellum
Can't consciously see, blindness	Occipital lobe
Can't remember the name of something; hard time reading	Parietal lobe
Problems moving body parts changes in personality	Frontal lobe
Trouble understanding what others are saying, short-term memory loss	Temporal lobe
Hard time swallowing or staying balanced	Brain stem

REMEMBER...?

Have you ever gone into a room, then forgotten why you went in there in the first place? Or, worse, forgotten how to do math problems during a test? Your brain's cerebrum is the storage place for all of your memories—bits of information that you process and save—but not all memories are the same. There's short-term memory, which holds small amounts of information for short amounts of time—like what you went into that room to do. Then there's long-term memory, which holds information from over half a minute to up to a lifetime. There are ways to move information from your short-term memory to your long-term memory, like when you study for a spelling test or when you memorize a new friend's phone number. It takes a conscious effort on your part to move that information between the parts of your brain responsible for memory.

Sometimes your memory isn't forever, though. Some information is lost as you age, and some information is lost when you don't use it for a while. Do you remember last year's spelling test words?

BAM! DID YOU JUMP?

Sometimes your brain or spinal cord reacts to something so fast, you don't even have time to think about it—like when someone drops a pile of books in a quiet library, you jump. Or when someone whips a ball right at you, and your hand flies up and catches it before you can think (or you duck!). That's because of something called reflexes—your brain or spinal cord fires a lightning-fast message to a part of your body that needs to respond, fast.

DID YOU KNOW?

Our prefrontal cortex is the best developed among all animals, which is why we are different than apes or gorillas! It allows us to think better, concentrate harder, and socialize with each other.

Sometimes your reflexes are learned, like when the ball comes flying at you. You've learned in the past that if you don't do something, like catch it or duck, you'll experience pain when it hits you. So you've taught your body to react very fast when it sees that ball coming at you. Other times, reflexes are things you can't even control, like when the doctor taps on the tendon just below your knee cap with the little mallot. Your lower leg jerks forward on its own, and you couldn't stop it if you tried. That's an automatic reflex. Your body mostly uses reflexes to protect you from injury (real or imagined).

MAKE YOUR OWN REACTION TESTER

Your brain performs faster than you can even realize. Sometimes your brain works all by itself (like with reflex reactions). Test your reflexes and watch how you can teach your brain to react faster.

1. Run the masking tape along the ruler. Divide it into six equal portions (measure and mark with lines). Number each segment.

2. Now, get a friend to help. Your friend will hold the ruler vertically with one hand by the upper edge. Keep the number one position at the bottom. Position the fingers of one of your hands at the bottom of the ruler, below the number one position. You shouldn't be touching the ruler, just have your hand ready.

3. Ask your friend to let go of the ruler suddenly, without asking you. Your job is to try to "pinch" or catch the ruler as it slips between your fingers, before it hits the floor.

4. Make a note of the number you catch the ruler at.

5. Repeat the experiment several times. See how fast you can get at catching the ruler.

6. What's happening? As your brain begins to figure out how fast the ruler will fall, it sends a message to your fingers more and more quickly. This should improve your time every time the ruler is dropped.

SUPPLIES

- masking tape
- ruler
- marker
- a friend

MAKE YOUR OWN "SEEING IS BELIEVING" EXPERIMENT

Your brain works together with your senses to interpret the world around you. Sometimes, your brain wants to understand something that doesn't make sense to it. Try this food experiment to see if you can convince your brain otherwise.

SUPPLIES

- corn
- rice
- piece of chicken
- food coloring in different colors

1. Cook the food until it is warm and ready to eat. Then, using a few drops of food coloring, color the food a different color than it usually is. Try coloring the corn green, the rice purple, and the chicken blue.

2. Arrange the food on a plate. Close your eyes and smell it (warm it back up if it's gotten cold as you colored it). Does it smell as good as it usually does? Would you eat it? Now open your eyes again. Does it appeal to you? Would you eat it if you couldn't smell it, just see it?

3. To take it a step further, ask a friend or family member to close their eyes before you bring the food out. Ask them if it smells good, and if they'd eat it. Then let them open their eyes and give you their opinion.

4. Your nose may be telling you that the food will be delicious—but your eyes, accustomed to seeing the food look a different color, may be telling your brain something different. What if you'd dyed the food gray? How appetizing would that be?

5. Professional chefs know that you first "eat" food with your eyes. That's why they spend quite a bit of time "plating" the food—arranging it so it looks just as wonderful as they hope it tastes.

CHAPTER 9
SENSES

ext time you go swimming, close your eyes, plug your ears, and go underwater. You'll still feel the water, but other than that, you won't be able to see, hear, smell, or taste. You've shut off four of your five main senses. You've lost most of your connection to the outside world. Lonely, isn't it? Your five senses help you keep in touch with the world you live in.

When an image enters your eye and passes through your lens, it's flipped upside down and "projected" onto the retina in the back of your eye. The message is passed through your optic nerve to your brain—and your brain figures out that it needs to flip the image "right side up" in order to understand it.

Even when you're not focusing on something in particular, your body is still receiving input, like feeling the pressure of the couch against your body, or hearing a dog barking outside in the distance, or smelling the loaf of banana bread your mom is pulling out of the oven. Those are your senses at work, processing input from all around you. When you focus on something, like when you read a book, listen to music, or taste a soup you've never tried before, you're consciously using your senses, too.

But you've got more senses than you think. Beyond smelling, hearing, tasting, feeling, and seeing, you've also got the senses of pain, balance, and temperature. All of these are ways your body's sense organs receive information from the outside world and relay it to your brain. Sensing the world can be enjoyable—like when you taste ice cream—but it can also be critical to your safety, or even your life. If you see a ball flying right at your head, you can get out of the way (fast!). Or, if you hear a car coming up the road behind you while you're on your bike, you can move over farther on the shoulder of the road. Without your senses, you'd be at great risk of injury.

Your sense organs receive a message—you see the ball or hear the car—and they convert that information into the tiny electrical charges that travel along sensory nerves to the brain, where the brain sorts out the information and interprets it, so you can respond accordingly.

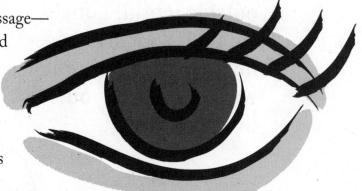

DID YOU KNOW?

A California boy, blind since age three, taught himself to use sound to "see" objects around him. He uses his tongue to make clicking sounds that bounce off objects—a technique called echolocation, used by dolphins and bats.

SEEING IS BELIEVING

Your eyes are like ping-pong balls that rest in the sockets formed by your skull. They're not hollow like ping-pong balls, though. They're filled with a squishy gel that helps them hold their shape. Muscles hold your eyes in place and help you roll them all around in their sockets, so you can look right, left, up, down, and cross-eyed.

The part of your eye that gives you your eye color is called the iris, and the little black center is your pupil. Your pupil lets in the light that you need to see. Muscles pull it open wider when you're in a dark theater and you need all the light you can get to see. When you're at the beach and the sun is gleaming bright off the sand, the muscles squeeze your pupil smaller because you don't need all that light in order to see.

Once your pupil has let the light inside your eye, it falls on a light-sensitive layer in the back of your eye called the retina. It's covered with cells that send tiny electrical messages to your brain to start interpreting what you're seeing.

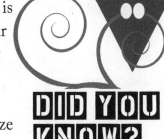

DID YOU KNOW?

Your eye muscles let you move your eyes around without moving your head, but an owl has to move its entire head to look around!

OPTICAL ILLUSIONS

You can trick your eyes with optical illusions. Here's a simple one: Hold your hands in front of you, with your index fingers pointing at each other. Keep them about an inch apart—don't let them touch each other! Holding them at eye level, look past them at a blank wall. You'll see a "mystery finger" with a fingernail on each end floating between your fingers!

Here's another one: Take a paper towel roll and hold it up to one eye like a telescope. Then hold your other hand, palm facing you, up against the side of the paper towel roll. Keep both eyes open. It will look like your hand has a hole right in the middle of it!

These tricks work because your eyes are combining two images together at the same time. Your brain is still seeing each image, but blending them together.

CAN'T SMELL THAT SMELL?

Ever wonder how people can be around smelly things, like garbage or rotting fish, and not seem to notice? That's because they've become **desensitized** to the smell. When an odor is present for an extended period of time, the receptors in your nose start to ignore them. You'd have to leave the smell for a little while and return to it before you could really smell it again.

The light that enters the eye has to be focused so that we can see sharply both near and far. The lens (a clear structure behind the pupil that is shaped like a lentil) does this active focusing. When the lens is focusing on something close-up, muscles make the lens thicker. If something's far away, those muscles make the lens thinner. By making the lens thicker, your eye is bending the light rays to focus on the retina so you see things clearly.

WORDS TO KNOW

desensitize: to lose your sense of something.

olfactory cells: nerve cells in your nose that help you pick up odors.

WHAT'S THAT SMELL?

Your nose is part of your respiratory system, but it also lets you get a whiff of the air around you, sometimes for better or for worse! Your sense of smell can bring pleasure, like when you catch a whiff of your favorite dessert baking in the oven. But it can also alert you to danger, like when there's a gas leak, or smoke from a fire.

What exactly is an odor? Think about the smell of brownies. The brownie "smell" is actually a bunch of tiny molecules that leave the brownies, floats through the air, and is inhaled by your nose. Your nose contains special nerve cells, called **olfactory cells**, which catch these odor molecules from the air. Then these cells send tiny electrical messages to your brain, which decodes these messages and says, "Brownies, yum!"

DID YOU KNOW?

Animals, like your dog, can smell far better than you can. While you smelled a cake baking in the oven, your dog could smell each of the ingredients and know it was made with raisins, nuts, sugar, and flour. That's because a dog's nose is packed with hundreds more smell receptors.

Have you ever smelled something that brought back strong memories? This happens to everyone. Scientists are still exploring why. One theory is that it's because the olfactory nerve in the brain is so close to the parts of the brain that control emotions and memory.

TASTE TEST

Your tongue does all the tasting, but it's actually quite limited. It can only detect four basic flavors: sweet, salty, bitter, and sour. Fortunately, your sense of taste is closely linked to your sense of smell, which enhances taste. When you get a good whiff of hot apple pie, your brain interprets that smell as something delicious. When you actually put a piece in your mouth, you're combining your tongue's input with your nose's. Yum! That's why when you've got a cold and your nose is stuffed, it's much harder to enjoy the taste of your food—you're only getting half the enjoyment.

When you eat food, your saliva starts to break it down and carries the flavors to your taste buds, which cover your tongue. Taste buds then send messages to your brain about the flavors you're eating. In addition to the four basic flavors, your tongue can also sense spiciness, the temperature of foods, and metallic tastes.

DID YOU KNOW?

Some people can't smell at all, because their olfactory cells have been damaged by physical injury or by toxic fumes.

TOUCHY, FEELY

You have touch, or sensory, receptors, all over your body. But some parts of your body have a higher concentration of receptors than others. For example, your fingertips have sensory receptors very close together. That's why you can feel very small differences in texture with them. But on your back, the sensory receptors are farther apart. Try having someone touch your back lightly with one finger. It's hard to identify exactly where they're touching you, isn't it?

Not all sensory receptors are alike, either. Some receptors feel pressure, others feel heat, and others feel cold. There are also sensory receptors for pain. They respond very quickly to a threatening stimulus. For example, if a pin pricks you, your pain receptors fire off a message to your brain, making you jerk your finger away to safety.

You probably think it would be nice to be able to turn off these pain receptors. But doing that could actually harm you, or even kill you! Pain alerts you to danger. How else would you know if you were touching a burning stovetop? Or if you had stepped on a nail?

ROUND AND ROUND

Why do you feel dizzy when you spin around quickly? It's because of your ears. In your inner ear are three almost circular chambers filled with liquid. Each chamber has tiny hairs growing in it. As you move, the fluid swishes around and bends various hairs. These hairs then send messages to the brain that tell your brain exactly how you are moving your head. This is part of your sense of balance.

But when you spin around, the fluid splashes crazily all over the hairs and your brain gets confusing information. It has trouble correcting your balance and you feel dizzy.

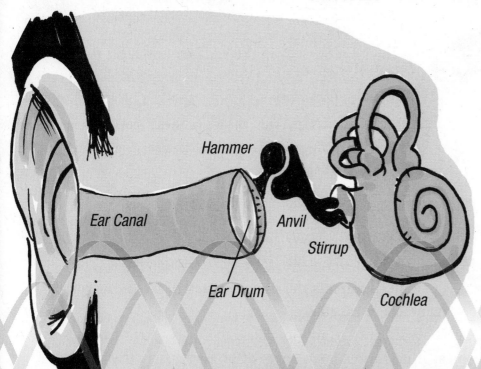

Hammer

Ear Canal

Anvil

Stirrup

Ear Drum

Cochlea

The hammer, anvil, and stirrup are the smallest bones in your entire body!

LISTEN TO THIS

You can't see sound, but you can sure hear it. When your parents call your name, for example, they're really sending out invisible vibrations called **sound waves**. These sound waves travel through the air. Your ears catch these vibrations and funnel them into the rest of your ear.

That's why your outer ear—the part of your ear you can see—looks the way it does. It's shaped like a cup so it can catch as many sound waves as possible. Try holding your hands around your ears to make an even bigger cup. Can't you hear even better now? That's because you're catching more sound waves.

After your outer ear catches the sound waves, it sends them along a channel called the ear canal. The sound waves then hit your ear drum, a thin membrane that really acts like the skin of a drum. What happens when you hit a drum—it vibrates, doesn't it? The same thing happens to your ear drum when sound waves hit it.

WORDS TO KNOW

sound waves: invisible vibrations in the air that you perceive as sound.

cochlea: the part of your ear where sound waves are turned into electrical signals and sent to your brain, for hearing.

The vibrations from the ear drum then hit three little bones. These tiny bones are named after their shapes: the hammer, anvil, and stirrup. The vibrations run through these bones in a chain reaction and continue on their way. Next stop—the **cochlea**.

The cochlea is shaped like a snail's shell. It's also filled with fluid. Here, in the fluid, the vibrations from sound waves are turned into electrical signals that are sent to your brain. Your brain interprets the signals and then you hear your name being called!

While your senses of taste and smell use chemical reactions, your ear is all mechanical. That means it's a series of physical parts that work together, like a chain reaction, to receive sounds.

When one or more of those parts becomes damaged in some way, your ear can't process sound any more—and you become deaf. You can lose your hearing because of a disease, an accident, or from something like listening to loud music through headphones.

DID YOU KNOW?

Seasickness occurs when your body becomes disoriented by the constant movement around you. Your eyes can't focus on one thing and your balance is thrown off, and as a result, you feel confused and sick.

MAKE YOUR OWN INDOOR SENSORY GARDEN

Grow plants that will tickle many of your senses with this plant project.

1. If you're not using a planting pot, poke a few holes in the bottom of your container and set it on a tray or put it outside. This way, your plants won't be sitting in soggy mud when you water them.

2. Put a thin layer of stones on the bottom of the pot to help with drainage.

3. Fill your container with soil and plant your seeds or seedlings. Group all the seeds of one kind together, instead of mixing all the different types together, so you'll really be able to see each kind.

SUPPLIES

- a large container for growing such as a pot, or any large waterproof container, depending on how big you want your garden
- small stones
- soil
- seeds or seedlings for plants (see list of suggestions)

Suggested Plants:

- **Smell:** mint, basil, lemon grass, or any type of herb
- **Sight:** colorful ivy, any small flowering plant
- **Touch:** cactus, aloe, lamb's ear
- **Taste:** cherry tomatoes, herbs
- **Sound:** grasses that rustle when you blow on them

MAKE YOUR OWN 3-D IMAGES

Your eyes can see in three dimensions because of their placement on your face. Using a little technology trick, you can make a flat image look like it's three-dimensional. You'll need to download a free program from the Internet, so be sure you have your parent's permission.

SUPPLIES

- poster board
- scissors
- blue and red film, also called acetate. You can find this at a craft store, or look around for a food item that's wrapped in blue or red clear wrappers. Sometimes candy is wrapped in it—you don't need a lot, just enough to cover your eyes.
- digital camera
- computer with Internet access (ask your parents for permission!)

1. Photocopy the pattern (on the next page) for the glasses, trace it onto the poster board, and cut it out. Don't forget to cut out the eye holes, too.

2. Tape the red film by its edges over the left eye hole and the blue film over the right eye hole. You've just created your 3D glasses! Set them aside.

3. Using the digital camera, take two photos of the same object. Take your time, and do this carefully—but here's the trick: After you take the first photo, stay in exactly the same position, except move the camera one or two inches to the left and take the second picture. Be sure to keep the camera at the same height—and move only the camera, not you. For the best results, take a picture of your subject with some stuff in the background, so you'll really get the full effect of three dimensions. (Try several different subjects, too, so you can play around with it and see what looks best.)

4. Download your photos onto the computer.

5. Next, you'll need to download a program that will let you create the image. There's a free one called Callipygian 3D; you can find it at http://www.callipygian.com/3D.

6. Open the program. You'll see two windows.

7. Under the menu that says "Selection Styles," select "Arbitrary."

8. Under the File menu, select "Open" and choose the image you took first for the right image, and the picture you took second for the left image.

9. Using the mouse, click and drag to select the area on the left photo that you want to be 3D—your subject. Then, under the View3D menu, choose Anaglyph.

10. Choose "Save 3D View" under the File menu.

11. When you open your file, put on your 3D glasses, and you'll see your photo in 3D!

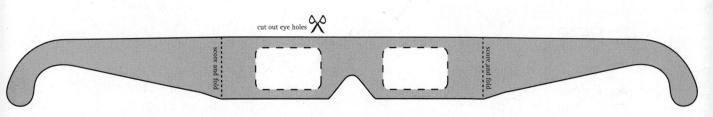

cut out eye holes

score and fold

score and fold

Photocopy this pattern for the glasses.
The image will need to be enlarged on a copier machine to fit on a child's face.

MAKE YOUR OWN OPTICAL ILLUSIONS

Here's another way to trick your eyes. In this project, your eyes will be sending a message to your brain, and your brain will be interpreting those messages in a way that's not really true!

SUPPLIES

- paper
- ruler
- colored markers and pencils
- math compass

1. For the first optical illusion, you're going to draw four rows of five colored squares. Using the ruler, draw a two-inch line, then skip ½ an inch, then draw another two-inch line. Do this five times. Make sure you don't move the ruler. The boxes will need to be exactly the same.

2. Return to your first line. Position the ruler at a right angle to the first line segment. Draw a two-inch line down (you're starting to draw the left side of the first box). Continuing to go downward, skip ½ an inch, then draw another two-inch vertical line. Repeat this two more times (you'll have four line segments).

3. Return to your first half-drawn box. You can now finish this box by drawing the bottom (two inches long) and the right side (two inches long). Continue working your way until you've drawn all 20 boxes.

4. Color the boxes all exactly the same color.

5. When you're finished, take a look at the results. Do you see black (or gray) dots at the crossing points between each square? You sure didn't draw those!

6. Here's what's happening: the sensors in your eyes are still receiving images from the colored squares, and the neurons are firing, even where there isn't anything to send the message (the empty spaces between the squares).

Here's another one:

1. Using the math compass, draw a circle on the paper. Color it in blue.

2. Around the circle, draw a big rectangle (so the circle will be in the middle of the rectangle). Fill in the rectangle with black. Be sure you don't color in the blue circle!

3. Now, stare at your picture for thirty seconds. Then, immediately look at a blank piece of white paper. What do you see? (Try blinking your eyes several times to see it better.)

4. Your black-and-blue picture has turned white and red! That's because when you stare for a long period of time, some of the color-detecting cones begin to tire out in your eyes. When you look at the blank paper, the other cones take charge and "show" you the other colors.

5. You can also do this with the American flag. Draw the flag, then color the stripes black and blue. Color the star field yellow. When you stare at it then look away, you'll see the familiar red, white, and blue!

And one more:

1. Using the math compass, draw a very small circle in the middle of your paper. Then, draw another circle around that one. And then another. Continue drawing circles ("concentric circles") until you've got about 15 or so. The closer you make the circles and the more evenly spaced they are, the better this will turn out.

2. When you're done, take a look at your drawing. If you jiggle the paper even a little, it will look like your circles are spinning around and around.

3. This illusion works because as you're looking at the picture, your nerve signals are "flashing" over the lines and the white spaces, turning the signals to your brain on and off. Your brain thinks this turning on and off is really movement from the circles.

MAKE YOUR OWN MODEL EAR

You can see how your ear receives sound through fluid when you make this model ear.

1. Cut the bottom off the can using a can opener.

2. Stretch the plastic wrap over the bottom of the can, and rubber-band it firmly in place.

3. Cut four slits in the bottom of the straw, and then spread the tabs out a bit.

4. Fit the ping-pong ball against the tabs, and tape it in place.

5. Securely tape the other end of the straw to the middle of the plastic wrap on the coffee can.

6. Next, hold the can so that the ping-pong ball is just resting on the surface of the water. Have a friend make a noise into the air-filled coffee can and watch the water.

7. As soon as your friend makes the noise, the sound travels through your artificial "ear drum" to the ball, where the vibrations make the ball dance on the water's surface, making ripples. Test different sounds—not only louder and softer, but also higher and lower pitches and see what effect they have on the water. This is similar to how your ear works, catching sound vibrations and passing them along to the cochlea.

MAKE YOUR OWN SNIFFER TESTER

Although our sense of smell isn't anywhere as strong as a dog's, you can still sniff out a scent. Find someone to help you with this experiment.

1. Find a room to work in that's free of clutter. If you can, push furniture out of the way before you start.

2. Put a few drops of your scent onto the cotton ball. Then give it to your assistant. Tie the blindfold on, and ask your assistant to put the cotton ball on the floor somewhere. Get down on your hands and knees.

3. When the cotton ball has been placed, try to see if you can find it by sniffing your way to it. You may discover this is much harder than it looks!

4. Try different scents to see which you can smell best. Or, let your assistant leave a trail of cotton balls to see if you can follow them.

SUPPLIES

- cotton balls
- vanilla extract, hand soap, or other strong-smelling liquid
- blindfold
- assistant

CHAPTER 10
REPRODUCTION

Your body is an incredibly complex, amazing organism. It's much more complicated than anything human beings can make. And yet we do create life, often without even thinking about it. How?

Life is created through sexual reproduction. With this type of reproduction, the new organism shares traits from each parent. The new person isn't an exact copy of either parent, but rather gets an equal number of its traits from both—and is a unique individual.

DID YOU KNOW?

Another kind of reproduction is non-sexual, or "asexual," where a new organism is produced directly off of a parent organism, like when yeast "buds" off to create a new organism. In this kind of reproduction, the offspring is identical to the parent.

With sexual reproduction, the male and the female each donate a sex cell that join together. Once they've joined to form one special cell, the cell starts dividing into two cells, then dividing again and again, until it forms what's called an embryo (a future human!). When it's a couple of months old, it's called a fetus. All this happens inside the mother's body: The sex cells join in a tube from your mother's womb and the embryo and fetus grow inside the womb, which is also called the uterus.

Since the fetus can't eat or breathe on its own, the baby will get what it needs from the mother, receiving nutrients and oxygen from the mother's blood. Any waste products from the baby pass through its blood, back to the mother's blood, where they're soon removed from her body along with her own waste products.

During all this, the cells of the developing person continue to multiply and to turn into special cells—skin cells, blood cells, nerve cells, and so on, and the baby grows and develops. The entire process takes 40 weeks.

GOT GOOD GENES?

Unless you're adopted, it would be strange if you didn't look like one or both of your parents in some way. Maybe you have the same eyes or hair, or the same body type, or even the same facial expressions. This is because of **heredity**. Heredity is the passing on of traits from parent to child. But how does heredity happen?

The answer lies in your cells. Each cell in your body has a chemical message that is the same in all your cells, but unique to you as a person. The message is "written" in the language of genes. It's your genes that give

WORDS TO KNOW

heredity: the passing of traits from one generation to another.

chromosomes: special rods in the nucleus of our cells; they contain the DNA that makes up our genes.

HUMAN DE

‹ Week 4
- looks a little like a tadpole
- a tail is visible
- heart starts beating
- neural groove forms to becomes the spinal cord and brain

Week 7 ›
- embryo is about ½ inch long
- the tail is almost gone
- lungs begin to form
- hands have fingers, but there's webbing between them

‹ Week 5
- ears start to form
- arms and legs begin to form that look like little "buds"

Week 8 ›
- the formation of all organs has begun
- the limbs are beginning to move

‹ Week 6
- embryo is about ¼ inch long
- there are two eyes, one on each side of the head
- the brain has divided into sections, one of which is the cerebrum
- hands begin to look like flat paddles at the end of the short arms

Week 9 ›
- eyelids begin to cover the eyes
- facial features develop more clearly

VELOPMENT

‹ Week 10-13

- the face looks more human as the eyes are closer together
- eyelids are formed and are closed
- red blood cells start being produced

‹ Week 14-17

- fetus is about six inches long
- fine hair forms on the head
- bones become harder

‹ Week 20

- eyebrows and eyelashes appear
- nails appear
- mother can feel fetus moving
- heartbeat can be heard

Week 28 ›

- the eyelids can open and close
- fetus is about 15 inches

Week 32 ›

- body fat increases

Week 37-40 ›

- the fetus is fully developed (called "full-term") and ready for birth

the instructions for what color your hair or eyes are, for example. Your genes are packed into rods called **chromosomes**. Think of each chromosome as a chapter in a cookbook. And the genes are the individual recipes.

But what are genes and chromosomes made out of, exactly? It's a substance called DNA, which is short for deoxyribonucleic acid. If you looked at DNA under a microscope, it would look like a strand.

Remember—chromosomes, genes, DNA—all are located in the nucleus of each one of your cells. And each one of your cells has 23 pairs of chromosomes, half of which came from your mother and half from your father.

So, you really are made from equal parts of your mom and dad!

In the 1800s, a scientist named Gregor Mendel began studying inherited traits in pea plants. He found that when genes from both parents come together, one is sometimes stronger than the other. That's called the dominant gene. The other gene is still there, but it won't be displayed in the offspring. That's the recessive gene. The dominant gene will usually have more influence over that trait. The gene for brown eyes is dominant over that for blue (or green) eyes.

There are many dominant and recessive traits that mix and match to create unique humans. But there are also diseases that hitch a ride on recessive genes, too—and those can be far more serious than guessing what color eyes a baby will have. Scientists study genetics to help uncover some of the secrets of these serious gene combinations.

CATCH THAT CROOK!

Scientists can use DNA to catch criminals, too. Because all of your cells carry your special genetic identification, any cells you leave behind at the scene of a crime will spill the beans and identify you as the culprit. If criminals leave behind a strand of hair, a broken fingernail, or even dead skin cells, scientists can pull DNA from them and find out who the bad guy is. All they need is a sample of a suspect's DNA and they can match them together.

MAKE YOUR OWN INHERITANCE MODEL

Has anyone ever said, "You've got your grandmother's eyes!" or "Wow, you look just like your father!"? If so, it's because you've had some of that genetic information (genotype) passed down to you, and it's showing itself (phenotype). Build this model to see how traits get passed down over time.

1. Start by choosing two basic shapes, like a circle and a rectangle. Make one of each. (Don't make them too big; about an inch or two is fine.) These represent the parents. Set them at the top of your work surface.

2. Imagine that the parents had four offspring. Make these offspring by creating four new shapes, each with one kind of circle and one kind of rectangle. You could make one very large circle with a small rectangle, or a large rectangle with a small circle. Mix these combinations any way you want. Lay your four offspring creations in a row right below the two parent shapes.

3. Now imagine that two of those offspring find partners. Select two of the offspring, and give them each a partner—a new shape. One could be a triangle, and one could be a square, for example.

4. Set the partners next to the offspring they're paired with. If these new pairs had offspring, what would they look like? Create offspring for both new pairs by combining the circle/rectangle combo of the original offspring with the new shape of the partners. So, you may have a circle/rectangle/triangle combo. Put these "second generation" offspring in a row underneath. You can continue doing this on and on, bringing in new shapes.

5. Take a look at the "family tree" you've created. Do you see how certain traits could be passed down from one generation?

MAKE YOUR OWN DNA EXTRACTION

You can't see DNA strands with your naked eye (they're 400 times thinner than human hair!). But with this project, you can see "clumps" of DNA strands taken from plant cells.

SUPPLIES

- rubbing alcohol
- ½ cup of split green peas (or you can use wheat germ or onions)
- table salt
- one cup of water
- blender
- cheesecloth or other straining material
- large bowl
- clear liquid dish detergent (not powdered or opaque)
- glass
- meat tenderizer (must contain papain—check the ingredient list)
- thin wire (optional)
- microscope (optional)

1. About an hour before you start, put the alcohol in the freezer to get it really cold. In fact, the colder you can keep everything in this project, the better your results will be.

2. Put the peas, a pinch of salt, and the cup of water (cold!) into the blender, and blend on high speed for about 20 seconds.

3. Lay several layers of cheesecloth over the empty bowl. You may want to have someone help hold it, or use rubber bands. Pour the mixture from the blender through the cheesecloth and into the bowl to strain it.

4. Squirt two tablespoons of dish detergent into the bowl and mix gently. You don't want it to get all foamy, so be very gentle. Mix for about two minutes.

5. Let this sit, untouched, for about five minutes.

6. After five minutes, carefully fill the glass halfway with the mixture, then add a pinch of meat tenderizer and gently stir for 15 seconds. Try not to get it too bubbly. If it gets too bubbly, you can very carefully blot at the bubbles with a paper towel to remove them.

7. Get the cold rubbing alcohol from the freezer and, pouring down the side of the glass so you don't disturb the mixture, add alcohol until the glass is just about full.

8. Let it sit for a couple of minutes. A white, stringy substance will form in between the layers of soapy mixture and alcohol—that's the peas' DNA. It's all clumped together, not in neat little strands like it is inside the cell nucleus. If you shape a thin wire into a hoop or a hook, you may be able to reach between the layers and lift many strands at once. See how long you can make them! If you'd like, look at them under the microscope. You should be able to make out little strings of DNA.

9. How did you get the DNA? When you put the peas in the blender, you broke open the cells of the peas. The dish detergent released the DNA from the nucleus by breaking down the cell membranes (just like it breaks down the fatty grease from dirty dishes). The papain in the meat tenderizer is an enzyme that breaks down proteins, so it releases the DNA from its surrounding proteins (and then the dish soap prevents it from sticking to them again). The DNA then moves toward the alcohol, away from the soapy mixture, but it can't enter the alcohol. That's why it's found in between those two layers.

10. You could even extract your own DNA. Just swish a mouthful of salty water in your mouth and spit it into a cup, then follow the same directions.

CHAPTER 11
DISEASES & IMMUNITY

When your mom says, "Wash your hands before dinner!" you may think it's because your hands are all dirty, and that may be true! But another reason why she wants you to wash your hands is because germs and bacteria that other people leave behind can hitch a ride on your hands— and into your body.

Once they get into your body, they can really cause some harm, making you sick. Fortunately, your body is a strong, tough fortress, and even simple actions like washing your hands in soapy water can prevent you from getting sick.

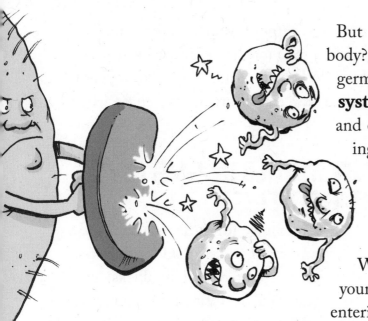

But what if something does enter your body? How can your body fight invading germs? It all starts with your **immune system**. This complex network of cells and organs is your defense against invading **germs** and **bacteria** that can make you sick. Different parts of your body work as a team to form your immune system. Your skin is a barrier that keeps stuff from entering your body. When you breathe through your nose, your nose hairs trap junk and keep it from entering your lungs. And your white blood cells can attack an organism that does get inside your body.

Bacteria are microorganisms that can be good or bad, depending on what kind of bacteria they are. Some bacteria are helpful to your body, like the ones in your intestines that help break down food. Others aren't—like Salmonella, a bacterium that gives you "food poisoning" and makes you sick to your stomach.

Germs and bacteria can get into your body in different ways. Suppose you get a cut on your finger. If you wash it well and cover it with an **antibiotic** cream and a bandage, you've made it harder for bacteria to get into your body—you've made a barrier and blocked its entry. But if you left the cut open and didn't clean or protect it, you may have left the door open for bacteria to come right in. Once it's in your body, it can jump into your bloodstream and maybe make you sick. If you've got a strong immune system, though, your body can fight the **infection**.

WORDS TO KNOW

immune system: the network of cells in your body that fight invading cells.

germs: microscopic organisms that can cause harm.

bacteria: microscopic, single-celled organisms.

antibiotic: something that destroys bacteria and other microorganisms.

infection: when microorganisms invade and make you sick.

Another way germs can enter your body is through your mouth or nose. If someone who's sick has germs on their hands, then touches a surface like a doorknob, some of those germs are left behind. When you come along and touch it, you could pick up some of them. Germs can also travel through the air, so when you breathe in, they can enter your body.

CHARGE! HOW YOUR IMMUNE SYSTEM GOES TO BATTLE

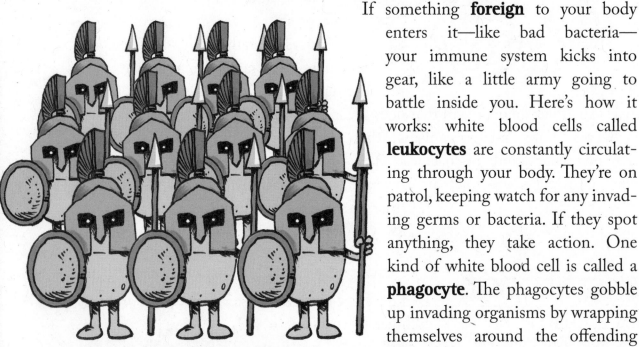

If something **foreign** to your body enters it—like bad bacteria—your immune system kicks into gear, like a little army going to battle inside you. Here's how it works: white blood cells called **leukocytes** are constantly circulating through your body. They're on patrol, keeping watch for any invading germs or bacteria. If they spot anything, they take action. One kind of white blood cell is called a **phagocyte**. The phagocytes gobble up invading organisms by wrapping themselves around the offending cells and destroying them.

DID YOU KNOW?

Phagocyte means "cell eater" in Greek.

Another kind of white blood cell is called a **lymphocyte**. These cells remember **antigens** that have invaded your body in the past, and help destroy them if they come back. When an antigen enters your body, your white blood cells find it and identify it. Then, the lymphocytes produce **antibodies**, special molecules that are made into a unique shape. Their shape lets them "lock on" to the antigens, like two puzzle pieces coming together.

Once the antibodies are locked into place a special kind of lymphocytes called T cells come to destroy the antigens. Phagocytes are also called into action, eating up the invaders.

After the invading cells are destroyed, you're healthy again. But your immune system doesn't just wait around for another invasion. Those antibodies stay in your system, on guard. If the same antigens try to invade, the antibodies and T cells remember them and prevent another infection. That's called **immunity**.

HEY, I DON'T FEEL SO GOOD...

Everyone gets a cold now and then. That's when a common **virus** infects your respiratory system, and you end up with a runny nose, sore throat, and a cough. Colds go away after about a week. But other kinds of illnesses can be more serious, last longer, and make you feel terrible, too:

* **Chicken pox** is a virus that causes red, itchy bumps all over your body.

* **The flu** shares some of the same symptoms as a cold, but it's a more severe virus. The **symptoms** of a flu are chills, fever, muscle pains, and feeling weak and tired all over.

WORDS TO KNOW

foreign: something that's not natural to your body.

leukocytes: white blood cells.

phagocyte: a white blood cell that destroys invading cells.

lymphocyte: a white blood cell that remembers prior infections.

antigen: a foreign molecule on a virus or a bacterium that invades your body.

antibodies: proteins that help the immune system fight infections or bacteria.

DID YOU KNOW?

Chicken pox got its name because people thought the bumps looked like chick peas were sitting on top of the skin!

* **Meningitis** is a very serious disease when the covering of your brain and spinal cord becomes inflamed. Symptoms are a very stiff neck, bad headache, and fever.

* **Allergies**—if someone can't eat peanuts or shellfish, for example—are actually your immune system overreacting to an antigen. You end up with an exaggerated immune response with watery eyes, sneezing, and swelling. Sometimes the response can be so severe it produces **anaphylaxis**, which is life-threatening.

GERMS SHOT DOWN

Nobody likes going to the doctor to get shots. But when you get shots called **vaccines**, you're helping build your immune system against diseases that could be deadly. Remember how your body recognizes organisms that have invaded it in the past? That's the way vaccines work. Vaccines are actual viruses and bacteria themselves, but they've been killed or weakened. When they enter your body, your immune system produces antibodies to fight and destroy the disease. Your immune defenses disable the germ and knock it out. After the disease is defeated, the antibodies stay in your system, and you're immune from that disease. That's why vaccines are also called immunizations.

Some of the most common vaccines protect against:

* **Measles** are an infection that gives you a rash, fever, and cough.

* **Mumps** cause a swelling of your salivary glands. It also gives you a fever and headache, and can lead to meningitis.

* **Rubella** is another serious infection that gives you a rash and swelling of your neck glands. It's also called German measles.

* **Tetanus** can make your muscles spasm tightly.

* **Pertussis** (sometimes called "whooping cough") gives you very serious coughing.

* **Polio** can cause **paralysis**.

* **Diphtheria** is a disease that affects your heart and throat.

CARING FOR YOUR IMMUNE SYSTEM

Just like all your other body systems and parts, you have to take care of your immune system so it can take care of you. Fortunately, it's pretty easy to build up a strong immunity:

* **Sleep.** Scientists aren't sure why getting enough sleep boosts your immune system, but they do know that the less sleep you get, the more likely you are to get sick.

* **Exercise.** When you exercise, you help your white blood cells produce chemicals that are natural opponents of diseases like cancer. You also increase the amount of white blood cells called "killer T cells." These cells seek out and destroy abnormal cells, keeping you healthy.

* **Eat well.** Munching on natural foods like fruits, vegetables, and whole grains (things like whole wheat bread or oatmeal) keeps your entire body strong and healthy. Your immune system in particular works best when you have plenty of vitamins and minerals from "super foods" like blueberries, oranges, garlic, and broccoli.

WORDS TO KNOW

immunity: when you can't get a certain disease.

virus: an infectious agent that causes disease.

symptoms: the signs of a disease, like red bumps or coughing.

anaphylaxis: a reaction to an antigen that causes life-threatening symptoms, like welts, difficulty breathing, and shock.

vaccine: a virus that is put into the body so antibodies that can kill it are created.

paralysis: when you're unable to move.

MAKE YOUR OWN BALL SOAP

You know staying clean helps your body fight germs. Here's a way to make a fun soap that you can use to wash up.

SUPPLIES

- leftover bits of soap—try to get a bunch of different colors
- liquid hand soap
- microwaveable bowl
- microwave

1. Put a bunch of soap bits in the microwaveable bowl.

2. Microwave for about ten seconds, until everything is warm and very soft, but not runny.

3. Put a little squirt of liquid hand soap in your hands, then gather up a small amount of the melted soap.

4. Squeeze the soap together into little balls. After they've hardened you can put them in a bowl by the sink.

MAKE YOUR OWN IMMUNITY SLUSH DRINK

When you eat foods that are high in vitamins and minerals, you help your immune system build up the strength it needs to fight invading bacteria. Here's a recipe that's loaded with vitamin C to help keep you healthy.

1. Put all the ingredients in a blender.

2. Blend until the everything's mixed and the drink is slushy.

3. Drink and stay healthy!

SUPPLIES

- 2 tablespoons lemon juice
- 1 cup crushed ice (or whole ice, if you've got a strong blender)
- ¼ cup frozen apple juice concentrate

GLOSSARY

anaphylaxis: a reaction to an antigen that causes life-threatening symptoms, like welts, difficulty breathing, and shock.

antibiotic: something that destroys bacteria and other microorganisms.

antibodies: proteins that help the immune system fight infections or bacteria.

antigen: a foreign molecule on a virus or a bacterium that invades your body.

aorta: the large artery carrying blood from the heart.

appendicular skeleton: arm and leg bones.

atria: chambers of the heart that receive blood from the veins.

atrophy: when muscles get smaller and weaker.

axial skeleton: the ribs, backbone, skull, and sternum.

bacteria: microscopic, single-celled organisms.

bolus: the soft blob of chewed food that you swallow.

bone marrow: the middle of the bone, which is soft and fatty.

carbon dioxide: the gas that's produced as a waste product by your body.

carbon monoxide: a colorless, odorless, very toxic gas that is in cigarette smoke.

cartilage: stiff, flexible tissue that mostly converts to bone in adults.

cell membrane: the cell's thin outer boundary.

chromosomes: special rods in the nucleus of our cells; they contain the DNA that makes up our genes.

cilia: tiny "hairs" that line your trachea.

clot: the clump of blood proteins and cells that's formed over a cut to help stop the blood flow.

cochlea: the part of your ear where sound waves are turned into electrical signals and sent to your brain, for hearing.

compact bone: the white, hard, outer part of bones.

concave: curving inward.

contraction: a tightening of your muscles.

cytoplasm: the jelly that fills the cell.

deoxyribonucleic acid (DNA): the substance that carries your genetic information, the "blueprint" of who you are.

dermis: the thick layer of the skin below the epidermis.

desensitize: to lose your sense of something.

enamel: the protective outside layer on teeth.

epidermis: the outer layer of the skin.

esophagus: the long tube connecting your mouth to your stomach.

fibrils: thin threads that make up muscle fibers.

foreign: something that's not natural to your body.

fracture: another name for a broken bone.

genetic: related to the origin of something; things about you that are passed from parent to child.

germs: microscopic organisms that can cause harm.

hemoglobin: the protein that carries oxygen in your bloodstream.

heredity: the passing of traits from one generation to another.

hormones: chemicals that travel through the bloodstream to signal other cells to do their job in the body.

immune system: the network of cells in your body that fight invading cells.

immunity: when you can't get a certain disease.

infection: when microorganisms invade and make you sick.

lamellar bone: a strong, hard type of bone material.

leukocytes: white blood cells.

ligaments: elastic tissue that attaches bones to each other.

lymphocyte: a white blood cell that remembers prior infections.

mitosis: how a cell splits up.

motor cells: cells that carry messages from your brain to your muscles.

muscle memory: the process of your muscles remembering how to work.

nervous system: the parts of the body that receive and interpret stimuli and send responses.

nucleus: the part of the cell that holds your genetic information.

olfactory cells: nerve cells in your nose that help you pick up odors.

organelles: the tiny parts of a cell.

ossification: the process of bone formation with the help of minerals like calcium.

paralysis: when you're unable to move.

parasites: an organism that feeds on and lives in another organism.

GLOSSARY

periosteum: the membrane on the outside of a bone.

peristalsis: the squeezing process of moving food through your esophagus, stomach, and intestines.

phagocyte: a white blood cell that destroys invading cells.

pharynx: the first part of your throat, right after your mouth.

pulmonary artery: an artery that carries poorly oxygenated blood from the right ventricle of the heart to the lungs.

ribonucleic acid (RNA): similar to DNA, RNA helps make proteins in your body.

sebum: the oily secretion of the sebaceous glands. With perspiration it moistens and protects the skin.

sedentary: not moving around much.

sensory cells: cells that carry messages from your sense organs to your brain.

sheath: a protective cover for your muscles.

sound waves: invisible vibrations in the air that you perceive as sound.

sphincter: a round muscle that opens and closes to let something pass through.

sternum: the wide, flat bone that joins your ribs together in front, also called the breastbone.

symptoms: the signs of a disease, like red bumps or coughing.

tendon: tissue that connects muscles to bones.

trachea: your windpipe, the tube through which air enters your lungs.

transfusion: transfer of blood from one person to another.

urea: waste product made from our cells.

ureters: tubes connecting the bladder to the kidneys.

vaccine: a virus that is put into the body so antibodies that can kill it are created.

vena cava: the main vein into the heart.

ventricles: chambers in the heart where blood is forced into arteries.

vertebrae: the bones that make up the spinal column.

virus: an infectious agent that causes disease.

RESOURCES

BOOKS

Ballard, Carol. *Lungs: Injury, Illness and Health.* Heinemann, 2003.

Brynie, Faith Hickman. *101 Questions About Blood and Circulation.* 21st Century, 2001.

Brynie, Faith Hickman. *101 Questions About Food and Digestion.* 21st Century, 2002.

Brynie, Faith Hickman. *101 Questions About Skin That Got Under Your Skin… Until Now.* 21st Century, 1999.

Brynie, Faith Hickman. *101 Questions About Your Immune System.* 21st Century, 2000.

Cole, Joanna. *The Magic School Bus Explores the Senses.* Scholastic, 2001.

Cole, Joanna. *The Magic School Bus Inside the Human Body.* Scholastic, 1990.

DK Publishing. *Skeleton.* DK Children, 2004.

DK Publishing. *The Human Body.* DK Adult, 1995.

LeMaster, Leslie Jean. *Cells and Tissues.* Childrens Press, 1985.

McPhee, Andrew T. *Sleep and Dreams.* Franklin Watts, 2001.

Parsons, Jayne. *Encyclopedia of the Human Body.* DK Children, 2002.

Seckel, Al. *The Art of Optical Illusions.* Carlton Books, 2000.

Simon, Seymour. *The Brain: Our Nervous System.* HarperCollins, 2006.

Simon, Seymour. *Guts: Our Digestive System.* HarperCollins, 2005.

Simon, Seymour. *Lungs: Your Respiratory System.* HarperCollins, 2007.

WEB SITES

KidsHealth. www.kidshealth.org/kid. Find out about the human body, learn how to stay healthy, and more.

Discovery Kids. www.kids.discovery.com. Visit the Grossology website and learn about some of the more unpleasant sides of human anatomy.

Dole Superkids. www.dole5aday.com. Find out how to make a balanced diet.

Kids Biology. www.kidsbiology.com. Explore the human body with an interactive website.

INDEX

INDEX